Books for Courageous Women

ESTHER PRESS VISION

*Publishing diverse voices that encourage and equip women to walk
courageously in the light of God's truth for such a time as this.*

BIBLICAL STATEMENT OF PURPOSE

*"For if you keep silent at this time, relief and deliverance will rise for the Jews from
another place, but you and your father's house will perish. And who knows whether
you have not come to the kingdom for such a time as this?"*

Esther 4:14 (ESV)

What people are saying about …

LIFE IS *Messy* GOD IS GOOD

"I've had the opportunity to speak with Cynthia Yanof many times about God's calling on our lives and how it's often masked in the most ordinary moments of everyday life. Faithfulness in the ordinary and finding God's presence in life's messiest moments are at the heart of *Life Is Messy, God Is Good*. I'm so grateful for a much-needed dose of laughter and biblical wisdom."

Mark Batterson, lead pastor and *New York Times*–bestselling author of *The Circle Maker*

"No one can make you laugh and praise Jesus within the span of just two sentences like Cynthia Yanof. In these pages, she reminds you that a messy life is normal. And even greater news: God is good and He is for you in the hard, devastating, and mundane moments. With witty stories and gospel truth, *Life Is Messy, God Is Good* will keep you moving forward with confidence, knowing the story isn't over yet. Thank goodness."

Heather MacFadyen, host of the *Don't Mom Alone* podcast, author of *Don't Mom Alone* and *Right Where You Belong*

"With her signature sense of humor, Cynthia Yanof scatters easy-to-gather, pocket-sized pearls of wisdom sure to help readers navigate life's inevitable messiness. In her "better together" style, she always has an open seat at her table for honest conversation and—the best part—she's happy to go first."

Kay Wills Wyma, writer, speaker, podcaster, author of *The Peace Project*

"Cynthia is one of those writers who always keeps things interesting. She is hilarious and will hit you with deep truths you weren't expecting. And just when you anticipate a deep dive, she'll touch you with a sentimental story that resonates with your soul because she is so real. She's great because she is an incredibly gifted writer. And she's better than great because she is an incredibly relatable woman."

Jonathan Pitts, president of For Girls Like You Ministries, pastor at Church of the City, speaker, author of *My Wynter Season*

LIFE IS
Messy
GOD IS
GOOD

CYNTHIA YANOF

LIFE IS
Messy
GOD IS
GOOD

SANITY FOR THE CHAOS OF EVERYDAY LIFE

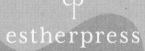

esther press

Books for Courageous Women
from David C Cook

LIFE IS MESSY, GOD IS GOOD.
Published by Esther Press,
an imprint of David C Cook
4050 Lee Vance Drive
Colorado Springs, CO 80918 U.S.A.

Integrity Music Limited, a Division of David C Cook
Brighton, East Sussex BN1 2RE, England

Esther Press®, DAVID C COOK®, and related logos are trademarks of David C Cook.

Library of Congress Control Number 2023939793
ISBN 978-0-8307-8533-9
eISBN 978-0-8307-8534-6

The Team: Susan McPherson, Stephanie Bennett, Judy Gillispie,
Leigh Davidson, James Hershberger, Susan Murdock
Cover Design: Micah Kandros

Printed in the United States of America
First Edition 2024

1 2 3 4 5 6 7 8 9 10

110623

This book is dedicated to my parents, Dorothy and Tom Wilkinson. It's impossible to appreciate the sacrificial love and intentionality required in parenting until you've lived it. Your dogged commitment to faith, joy, and walking alongside others has marked me.

"Generation after generation stands in awe of your work; each one tells stories of your mighty acts" (Psalm 145:4 MSG).

Contents

Introduction

A couple of my dearest friends and I decided to go to a "healthy eating" class several years ago.

Scratch that.

Let's agree from the get-go to be brutally honest and call it what it is. I'll start over.

A couple of my dearest friends and I decided to go to fat camp several years ago. A local church was offering a health-based Bible study on Thursday nights where we would examine food in light of biblical principles. It seems I hadn't been examining food based on any principle, hence the need to go to the class.

Somewhere about three weeks into our twelve-week study, I arrived at our round table a little bit late (literally it was round, not a reference to the shape of the participants). I quietly shimmied into the chair my sweet friends had saved for me and pulled out my book, ready to set the world on fire with my newfound resolve to eat better.

I sat across from one of my dear friends who made me promise I wouldn't mention her name in any context, much less in a literary work. So I won't. But it rhymes with Karen and starts with a "Sh."

It was a cold day at fat camp (literally and metaphorically), and my friend Karen was wearing a cute little scarf with her outfit. Just as I was admiring her fashion prowess, something caught the periphery of my eye. What was on her scarf—possibly an accessory on her accessory?

On further inspection—well, there're just no words. I lost it with one of those "I can't believe I'm laughing at a funeral" kind of laughs. The one when your spouse slips on the very tiniest patch of water on the bathroom floor, and you're giving it everything you've got not to laugh when he falls but just can't hold it in?

Or maybe that's just me.

Turns out my sweet friend was sitting there fabulously unaware she had a French fry stuck in her scarf.

A French fry at fat camp, God bless her.

Please don't miss the visual of this dear friend sitting there with readers on, diligently taking notes in an "I can do all things" kind of journal, completely oblivious to the fact she was harboring a fugitive French fry.

Oh, and for clarification, it was not a small sliver of a fry one might get at McDonald's. Nope, it was an honest to goodness Chick-fil-A waffle fry hanging out on her stylish scarf.

She later explained how she made the decision to go out with a bang and hit the drive-through as a pre-diet, dash-and-dine kind of thing. Let's be clear: there was absolutely no judgment from me other than the fact she didn't invite me to join her. After all, who of us hasn't eaten their way through a "pantry cleaning" all in the name of kicking off a diet tomorrow? Not to mention I live most of my life camped out in these same type of messy places hoping God can shape my mess into His greater message.

But if you aren't getting the humor of this, I'll have to assume you're either one of those "I forget to eat sometimes" kind of people or you eat only half your plate and claim, "It's just too rich."

I still love you as a sister in Christ, but I'm gonna have to try a little harder to make you my people.

My girls don't do that stuff.

There's none of that ordering the same thing I do and then eating just three bites before declaring "You're gonna have to roll me

out of here," all the while oblivious to the fact I've plowed through
the whole plate.

Likewise, my people also don't throw around weight-loss man-
tras like:

> "Nothing tastes as good as skinny feels." (Incorrect,
>   cheese fries.)
> "Change begins today." (Wrong, tomorrow after
>   Tex-Mex works too.)
> "Your body achieves what your mind believes." (My
>   mind believes in carbs.)
> "Three months from now you will thank yourself."
>   (Whatever, you're dead to me.)

The three of us lost it that night. It was a tears-rolling-down-
your-face kind of laughter that was downright therapeutic. Sure,
very few people joined us at our round table in the following weeks
(okay, nobody), but we walked away with a much-needed reminder
of the value of deep friendships, the healing power of a good laugh,
and the need for a little grace in the hard places where we miss the
mark.

Can you relate? Have you ever felt like you're trying to take
the next right step only to end up in life's drive-through craving a
French fry more than a Kardashian craves a reality show?

Me too.

Here's the irony: your French fry always gives you away. I know,
profound, right?

But seriously, what's on the outside all too often gives away what's really going on inside. And for many of us, what's on the inside—or lacking on the inside—becomes painfully visible to those with a clear view of the outside.

SO WHY DOES IT MATTER?

Simply put, God created us for great purpose in this life. Long before the earth was formed and before we took even one little baby breath, God knew every single detail of our lives. With great expectation, He laid the groundwork for us to live purposeful lives, drawing closer to Him while also pointing others to Jesus.

In Psalm 139:16, King David says it this way: "Your eyes saw my unformed body; all the days ordained for me were written in your book before one of them came to be."

In other words, God has great plans for us that He put into place before we were ever born. He uniquely created each of us with God-sized plans for our lives and perfectly equipped us to accomplish them with His strength.

Knowing this, can we stop here for one second to consider how our lives might be transformed if we lived each day with even the tiniest grasp of our immeasurable value?

What incredible impact might a series of small pivots have on our families, our workplaces, and even our communities if we would accept nothing less than a life marked by God's greater mission and purpose?

With great expectation, He laid the groundwork for us to live purposeful lives, drawing closer to Him while also pointing others to Jesus.

But to do that, we're going to need to name and acknowledge some of the most sacred places where things have become really hard in our lives. Those places that tempt us to move from trusting the One who holds our every breath to questioning His goodness and faithfulness.

Because, just as fast-food habits are a surefire way to thwart our best-laid diet plans, unacknowledged hard places in our lives can thwart God's best-laid plans for us.

So pardon me while I step on some toes for a quick moment, mostly my own:

Perhaps you struggle with insecurity and find yourself always trying to prove you're worthy, even when you know your identity should be in the Lord. You find yourself making decisions based on how they will look to others or if you will be perceived as successful.

You work to maintain certain appearances so people won't see the real struggles below the surface. You feel like it's not obvious, yet it shows up in how you use your finances, how you treat your spouse, how you parent, or how you allow others into your life. You spend time consumed with the need to prove who you are instead of resting in the One who is the I AM.

Or maybe you're overwhelmed with a sin in your past that keeps you from living fully in the Lord today. The enemy's messaging has convinced you that you're disqualified from the God things because of wrong decisions, past mistakes, and even current sin. You feel certain that if people knew the real you, they would scatter. God's blessings and kingdom plans are for "better" people—so you're living with the weight of disqualification instead of living in the freedom of God's forgiveness.

For many of us the issue may be pride. We feel like we've done things mostly right in life and we deserve the opportunities afforded us. We struggle with a lack of empathy for others who share their vulnerabilities because, after all, if we can get it done, why can't they? Yes, everything belongs to the Lord, and it's by His blessing we have what we do, but deep down we believe we deserve the blessings we have.

Or maybe it's jealousy, comparison, bitterness, self-sufficiency, anger, complacency, unmet expectations, or withheld apologies? Are you getting it?

Like my friend Karen, we all have places where extra baggage is clouding our decision-making, and we're left discouraged and striving for more when God just wants us to rest in His grasp.

Life is messy. Yes, it's messy, unpredictable, painful, sloppy, emotional, slippery, and oftentimes unbearable with hard places we could never have fathomed when we started this journey.

But God wants to use these very same messes to shape us and develop His greater message in us. He's not surprised by our slipups and screwups. He's for us and loves us, so let's slow down for a tiny second and reframe the hard places we're facing.

Let me net it out real fast: Life is messy, but God is good. Each day we are given the opportunity to live with meaning and significance as we acknowledge our struggles and then surrender them to Jesus. So let's walk through some messy places together and laugh as we do it.

But a warning from the esteemed Ricky Bobby: "Hang on, Baby Jesus, this is gon' get bumpy!"[1]

CHAPTER 1

A Little Oil Goes a Long Way

MESSY TRUTH

Nothing we strive for in this life will
last if God has not anointed it.

hen you're facing a crisis, it's always good to have someone who is levelheaded and rational on your side. A
person who knows when to speak, when to be quiet,
and who's loaded with wisdom that spills out at just the right
moment.

~~I'm totally that person.~~ I mean, I've always wanted to be that
person. Although most people would say I'm pretty levelheaded in
tense situations, my kryptonite is awkward silence. Even as I'm writing these words, when it feels like there's a slight pause I desperately
want to type randomness like: "My roots are getting grayer by the
minute, but my hair girl says 'You know what I mean' at the end of
every sentence, and if I go to her again, I'll gouge out my eyes."

You know what I mean?

It's a serious problem. I mean, not as serious as the health condi-
tions in underdeveloped nations or NATO's struggles with foreign
relations, yet it's still a problem. What's most troublesome is that I
don't fill the silence with great wisdom or quotable quips that send
people running for a pen and Grandma's Bible; instead, I blurt out
randomness.

Like when my daughter was having trouble ordering at an
Italian restaurant a few years back, and we all sat there awkwardly
waiting. The waiter was growing increasingly impatient, so I jumped
right out there with "She's got a weird lactose issue that bothers her,
especially with pizza. She's thrown up at most of the middle-school
sleepovers she's been invited to the last few years. We haven't tested
her for allergies or anything like that; it's just a rogue puke and then
she's good to go."

I know, it's rough.

Or there are those situations where my uncomfortable goes into full panic, and my attempts to be funny are anything but. One of those foot-in-mouth, fill-in-the-silence moments happened at a Halloween party we hosted years ago. I didn't really know the couple coming through the front door, so I nervously commented that the husband's mask was perfectly disgusting for a kids' Halloween party. His wife kindly let me know he had undergone a dermatological procedure that morning, and it wasn't a mask.

TO ANOINT OR NOT TO ANOINT—THAT IS THE QUESTION

My friend April called me several years ago with some devastating news. She had been diagnosed with a brain tumor, which was most likely malignant and difficult to treat. After a quick consultation with Dr. Google, I understood the gravity of this diagnosis and wanted to help her walk through this health crisis the best I could.

April and I have been good friends ever since we were college roommates. We're opposites in almost every way possible, but it still works. She's a CPA who is understated, calculated, and deliberate in how she does life. In college, she delicately balanced working part-time with exercising, eating well, and focusing on her studies. (I did not.) She has also known what she wants to accomplish from an early age and has purposefully and linearly worked toward her goals. (Again, I have not.)

So with more than twenty years of friendship under our belts, we agreed that it only made sense for me to be there for her family during this critical brain surgery. Or maybe I agreed to it and she would have preferred I stayed my five hours away but—tomato, tomahto—I was going.

The night before surgery, I overheard April and her husband discussing a call they'd received from their church elders asking to come over to pray for her and anoint her with oil. April and Rob had never been part of an anointing of this sort, and they were discussing their comfort level. Darn the awkward silence that resulted in me suggesting that one about to undergo a ten-hour brain surgery might have nothing to lose in accepting a little prayer and anointing.

They agreed to the request, and a short time later their church showed up. I mean *really, really* showed up. What I assumed would only be a few people turned out to be more than sixty believers standing shoulder to shoulder—literally and metaphorically—with April that evening. And what I anticipated to be a few dabs of oil and a quick prayer became so much more as the evening played out.

Ointment AND OTHER WORDS I HATE

Before we continue, I feel it's necessary to say that I struggle with the word *anointment* because it sounds like *ointment*. And it's not that I'm wholly against creams that treat itches and other precarious needs better left unspoken—it's more that ointment is on my banned-words list. Yes, there are certain words I will not tolerate, like *humongous, chunky, satchel, pubic,* and *ointment.* Now knowing these words are heinous and strictly off-limits, my friends attempt to use them as often as possible and typically in one sentence. I'll spare you examples of such immaturity, but let's move forward with an understanding that *anointment* and *ointment* are a little too close for comfort.

Now I'm no anointment expert over here, but I've read a lot about it in the Bible through the years. In the Old Testament, it was a ceremonial process signifying God's blessing or call on a person's life. Anointing with oil was reserved for priests, kings, or prophets who were set apart for a special purpose or some next step God was asking them to take. I think of God telling Samuel to go anoint David and formalize his calling as king.

Rick Warren describes anointing with oil as "an external anointing by people of an internal anointing by God."[1]

Of course, there are also the New Testament examples of using oil to anoint the sick or even a woman who was criticized for using expensive oil to anoint the feet of Jesus. But I always thought of anointing as an antiquated concept until I realized Jesus has anointed us even today (1 John 2:20; 2 Cor. 1:21–22). Practically speaking, that means we don't have to be named a priest, a prophet, or a king to be anointed because Jesus' personal calling on our lives is just as significant as any of those given in the Old Testament. What God was doing through anointment back then, He's still doing today with real and powerful purposes for our lives.

FOOTPRINTS ON THE HARDWOODS

After everyone left April's home the evening of the anointing, I noticed something unusual. You know how cooking oil is hard to get off your hands because it leaves a residue behind? Well, the anointing oil from April's head made it down to her feet. As she walked around the house, she left footprints everywhere she stepped. Her visible footprints on the hardwood floors forced me to joke that she might not want to rob a bank pre-op because she'd be easy to track.

#AwkwardSilenceProblems

But watching April walk around that night with oily feet taught me something important about my faith: *People who have been anointed by Jesus should be leaving footprints everywhere they go.*

Are you with me? God has anointed us to do important things that He planned for our lives long before we were ever born. Just as a priest, a king, or a prophet was anointed in the Old Testament to do big things, we too are anointed as parents, teachers, friends, accountants, and attorneys.

Our anointing is so much more than a little oil on the brow—it's the unmatched power and supernatural ability to do the things God has orchestrated for our lives. When we do what God has anointed us to do, people and circumstances around us are changed. Our footprints, like April's, are visible long after we've moved on because God is using us to change hearts, resolve conflicts, heal brokenness, and accomplish ministry.

But living in this way doesn't just benefit those around us; it changes our lives too. It's easier to extend forgiveness, offer second chances, and keep short accounts when we're wronged because it's no longer all about us but about God working through us.

When we do what God has anointed us to do, people and circumstances around us are changed.

Speaking of keeping short accounts, it reminds me of our early marriage finances. Mike and I dated for a small eternity before we got married (like seven years), so we already had jobs, bank accounts, 401(k)s, and all the adulting kinds of things. Once our nuptials were finalized, we began the process of combining households.

About six months into our marriage, we noticed that every month our joint bank account was overdrawn and pulling money from savings. Month after month we didn't have enough to cover our bills, and we couldn't understand how we had been financially stable as singles but financially strapped once married.

A few months later we clued in that, in our newlywed bliss, we had both set up auto-pay to cover our bills. That was real cute until month after month, we double paid our cars, our house, the electricity, the water, and so on. Yes, I realize the fact that it took us months to figure this out is a bit perplexing; that's why those who stink at math (and common sense) oftentimes go to law school.

But I'm reminded of how prone I am to live each day double paying debts that have already been covered on my behalf. Jesus paid our debts and gave us unmatched value, which allows us to live each day free from the expectations of this world. As we do so, we're able to focus on the things that are uniquely ours to accomplish while drowning out the noise of distraction, discontentment, and comparison.

This brings freedom.

This brings hope.

Even so, sometimes in the middle of doing the things God has anointed for our lives, we can get tricked into thinking they're mundane, irrelevant, or even insignificant in comparison to what God's doing in other people's lives. We start to feel ripped off when we're called to make dinner for a neighbor instead of influencing two million Instagram followers.

But I've found that God tends to wrap our greatest callings into the most common things of everyday life. And because of this, Anne Graham Lotz (Billy Graham's daughter) says we should make it our goal each day to simply "be faithful in our highest place of influence."[2]

The world as we know it would be totally unrecognizable if we would stop looking around at others and instead focus on living faithfully in our own highest place of influence.

What would this look like, practically speaking?

If my highest place of influence today is in my home, then I'm going to leave footprints teaching my children how to live humbly, follow God, and love other people well.

If my highest place of influence is on the PTA board this year, my footprints will model kindness and inclusivity, prioritizing people over programs no matter the cost.

If my highest place of influence is in my work, I'm leaving footprints of integrity and uncompromising ethics regardless of the impact on my finances or future.

Why?

Because nothing we strive to accomplish is significant if it's not from God.

Nothing we strive to accomplish will bear success without God's hand.

Nothing we strive to excel in will last beyond us if God has not anointed it in our lives.

SECOND CHANCES

I learned a lot from April's anointing all those years ago. I learned that the miracle of anointing is rarely in the oil but in the footprints that come after the oil. King David's legacy didn't magically happen because Samuel dabbed a little oil on his forehead; it happened in the moment-by-moment faithfulness of doing what God planned for his life, called him to do, and empowered him to accomplish.

Thankfully, April came through her ten-hour surgery remarkably well the next day. A few weeks later—to the surprise of the top neurosurgeons in the country—her brain tumor was benign. So, with a clean bill of health, April was free to go back to her normal life.

Well, kind of.

Turns out that normal looks different on the other side of a second chance. What mattered yesterday seems to hold less significance today. The calculated, balanced life before seems inconsequential when faced with the reality that our days are limited and they are not our own.

I want to live each day as one given a second chance. I want to revel in my spiritual clean bill of health while seizing the Old Testament-sized anointments God has given me to accomplish.

Don't settle for anything less than God's plans for your life. Refuse to be hoodwinked by comparison or feel disappointed by the size of God's call on your life. Ask God to renew His anointing for your life (like, really do it right now). And then watch carefully and wait patiently as the anointing oil leaves unmistakable footprints everywhere you go.

CHAPTER 2

Skating Rinks and Sweatshirts

MESSY TRUTH

In a world threatening to change my name for as long as I can remember, I choose to listen only to the name above all names.

*M*iddle school is a friend to no one.

I have no doubt about this, having recently watched my two older children navigate the complicated middle school years. It threw me right back into those puberty-starting, bra-shopping, acne-sporting, confidence-crushing days I've been trying to forget for the last thirty-plus years.

Hideous.

The only saving grace of my own middle school years is that they fell right in the heart of the 1980s. I think we can agree the 1980s were God's peace offering to those of us who long-suffered through the fashion and music of the 1970s. After all, the '80s lived its very best life by giving us Bon Jovi, Vans, leg warmers, crimping irons, blue eyeliner, *Pretty in Pink*, and my mom's special in-home perm skills.

I was living big all those years ago, tanning in the backyard with baby oil slathered about me and a little tinfoil piece behind the head. And please note the in-home perms reference above, and picture one's hair in the context of baby oil, tinfoil, and the extreme heat of West Texas. So yes, I was smokin' hot in my middle school years (said not one person ever).

But even the greatness of the '80s couldn't fully insulate one from the middle school shrapnel launched at every turn. As if walking the halls every day in sheer horror of when your period might strike wasn't enough, the opportunities for social devastation *flowed* into the weekend, courtesy of the skating rink.

Without bragging too much, I must share I looked pretty fabulous in my white skates with hot-pink custom wheels, gliding backward with my tightly permed hair blowing (as much as it possibly could) in the breeze. Yep, we were enjoying some good, clean fun until some overhyped rink DJ on a power trip decided to institute the SKLOW dance (i.e., skating slow dance; please keep up).

I spent Friday nights skating at the Time Tunnel, and the kill-joy slow dance to which I refer was called the snowball dance. I'm sure your local skating rink had something similar that went something like this: the lights slowly dimmed, bubble spotlights started to fly all over the room, and the music awkwardly slowed down, which immediately set off one's fight-or-flight response.

The girls would start to line up on one side of the rink with the boys on the opposite side. And in the most awkward of fashions, one boy after another would glide by and choose a girl from the wall for a spin around the rink. There we stood against the wall, desperately hoping the next boy skating by would pick us, all the while watching "that girl" get one skate-by ask after another.

I'm sure it was plenty romantic skating to "Faithfully" under the neon spotlights (while fifty-plus girls threw imaginary daggers at you from the side of the rink where they stood waiting). But I'll never know.

Thankfully, just when you were about to head over to the snack bar to lament over a giant pickle and some nachos, the lights came back on to the welcomed beat of "Love Shack." And just like that, we all piled back on the rink like nothing absurdly weird had just happened.

Who cares! It's over, and we survived another week of the dreaded snowball dance.

"Tin roof ... rusted!"[1]

Around the same time, somewhere in the mid-'80s, the neon craze hit my West Texas town of El Paso. We were way over Atari by that point (gag me, that was so 1970s), and the oversized neon sweatshirt was about as cool as it got. One particular Christmas, I was anything but subtle in making it known that my one must-have was a neon-pink sweatshirt with the year 1985 printed on it.

(Well, I also wanted a waterbed because my friend Staci had one and it was fantastic. I could all but taste the good life of cool water swishing beneath me while I listened to Duran Duran on my Walkman. But apparently Tom and Dorothy [the parentals] wouldn't even discuss the waterbed must-have, dismissing it with some rhetoric about how "some kids don't have any beds at all." Staci also had her own private phone line and, well, I just couldn't even.)

Thankfully, Tom and Dorothy didn't disappoint; on Christmas morning I finally got the poly-cotton blend of fabulousness in my hands. It was neon-pink fabulousness, that sweatshirt, with "1985" so boldly printed across the front.

And talk about being transitional before transitional even existed—I could wear that beauty with either my Guess or Jordache jeans. Shoot, I even had my jelly shoes coordinated to ensure I was fabulous from head to toe.

(If I might add, my older brothers called my jellies Dairy Queen baskets, and it was super offensive. Oh, and did you know that Benetton clothes are now sold online for quite a penny because they are "vintage"? I'm sorry eBay, but we're going to have to agree to disagree that items from the '80s qualify as vintage.)

Obviously (said like a Valley girl), I was beside myself wearing my sweatshirt to school the first day back from Christmas break. I paraded that sucker down the halls of my beloved Lincoln Middle School like it was my job. There was nothing and nobody gonna break my stride this day.

Well, almost nobody.

Shortly after lunch, when I was coming out of the library, I noticed a few older boys giving me the eye. I knew it was my sweatshirt, and I couldn't blame them for gawking at my fabulousness. I was my best self in that shirt.

Then one of them, referencing the "1985" written so boldly across my front side, had the audacity to ask if the number represented my weight.

Oh no you did not. Shots fired!

My witty retort went something like this: "No, that's actually a reference to your median income in a few years when you're flipping burgers."

Well, I didn't actually say this. I didn't actually say anything. But what I did do was beeline it home that day to burn that stinkin' sweatshirt, hoping not one person would remember it ever existed.

I'm still in counseling. It's fine. Whatever.

THE NAME ABOVE ALL NAMES

It's funny how the passing of time and a lot of gray hair (*always* highlighted) brings perspective and healing. As I look back now,

I can see how so many of my earliest memories are the very things that have shaped my identity in the best (and most difficult) of ways.

For example, there's literally no way for me to express my gratitude for the gift of a godly family who has unconditionally loved me from my very first breath and will do so until my very last. I'm completely humbled by the idea that every decision they have made has come from a place of intentionality and purposefulness because I hold great value to them.

But time has also allowed me to see how the proverbial skating-rink rejections and sweatshirt insults have also carved little paths to my soul that, left unattended, can make me feel overlooked, insignificant, or simply not enough.

Even as my parents picked my name with painstaking love and intentionality, there's a renaming in this world measured by the zip code of our homes, the size of our bank accounts, the choices of our kids, and the titles behind our names.

But God. He knows us to our deepest core and understands the nuances of our name-game struggles. We see it clearly when His Word defines Boaz as "strength," David as "beloved," and even Sarai as "contentiousness" (had to include that, bless it, with God giving you a name referencing your contentiousness).

Only God fully understands how these somewhat simple names hold immense significance because the very names reflect character, giftings, and the heart of the One who gave these names, loves them, and calls them His own. And instead of allowing a fallen world to rename those He loves and created in His image, He very literally steps in to change the names of His people so they might get small glimpses of who they are to Him.

But God. He knows us to our deepest core and understands the nuances of our name-game struggles.

I think of how He changed Abram's name to Abraham, renaming a ninety-nine-year-old barren man to "father of nations" to reaffirm a promise of what was to come. Or even Jacob, named "deceiver," was renamed Israel as a reminder that it's okay to wrestle out the very hardest of places when we do it with God.

Even if God hasn't literally changed my name this side of heaven, I know a new one is awaiting me. Revelation 2:17 says: "I will also give that person a white stone with a new name written on it, known only to the one who receives it." Only God knows our new names, and He will reveal them to us when we meet Him face to face for all eternity.

And don't miss the significance of the white stone in biblical times. Commentators tell us that receiving a white stone was equivalent to a winner of a competition (think: Olympic gold medalist) receiving an invitation or ticket to attend a grand celebration or banquet in his honor. The white stone was also used in the judicial system when a judge deemed the accused not guilty.[2]

In a world that has threatened to change my name for as long as I can remember, I choose today to listen to the only One who has extended me an invitation into my Savior's great banquet and declared my innocence through His own blood on the cross at Calvary.

We will always have those days when we're called "1985" or skated past during the snowball dance, but in those very skating rinks and school halls and marriages and jobs, and in raising kids and in tough friendships … the name above all names calls out to you and to me and reminds us of our true name: His.

CHAPTER 3

Answering the Call

MESSY TRUTH

Loving what God loves means caring about
the things we would prefer to sweep under
the rug and stepping into stories we've
become comfortable overlooking.

*T*here are certain things you prepare for all your life, but when they happen, nobody is more surprised than you. Like getting into a certain college, landing your first job, or applying self-tanning lotion evenly on your knees and elbows.

You spend months or even years preparing for these milestone moments, and then you're like "wait, what?" when the dominoes start falling into place.

I've found the same thing applies when we get serious about our faith. We spend a lifetime reading about Jesus, praying, and asking Him to show us the best way to live each day. But we're left speechless when He reveals His unique plans for our lives, and even more caught off guard when they don't line up with our own.

Or at least that's what happened to me.

A RELUCTANT YES

I was sitting in my office one afternoon when out of nowhere I had this deep feeling that God was calling me to something more for my life. I felt Him stirring up something I had never felt before, which was unusual because I'm not one who regularly recognizes signs from God or sees Jesus' profile on a slice of toast.

I realized I was experiencing that feeling of "holy discontent" that I'd heard about all those years ago growing up in the church. And although I couldn't pinpoint the feeling in the moment (and was hoping a few Tums would do the trick), deep down I knew God was asking me to move in a new direction with my life.

And so, right there on the thirty-fifth floor of a downtown Dallas law firm, I laid my head back in my chair and prayed a simple and somewhat unremarkable prayer: *Lord, I'll do whatever You're asking me to do if You will just make the path obvious and protect my family in the process.*

True to form, God began revealing His plans, and within a few months Mike and I knew He was calling our family to make some changes in order to free ourselves up for foster care. Can we be honest here for a hot minute? There's nobody out there thinking, *Hey, let's dabble in foster care. That sounds both convenient and fun!*

Nope, it's a well-established hard road paved with brokenness and suffering. Not to mention it's also one of those places I had always assumed only the truly hard-core Christians got involved with. (We're more of the types whose calendars are often over-booked making our lives under-spiritual.) Heck, we even let our kids play select sports some Sundays and still haven't finished watching *The Chosen*, so surely God was way off asking us.

Yet, with upward of four-hundred thousand children in the United States foster care system, we were convinced it was time for our family to practice what we preach and do our part to love and care for precious children who need a place to call home. And so I traded in the mounds of paperwork from my law practice for the mounds of paperwork from the state, and we were off to the races to become licensed foster parents.

Clearly we're dullards in my house, as one would think that the thirteen months of classes, background checks, home studies, and CPR certifications would have prepared us for that middle-of-the-night phone call just hours after becoming licensed. Yet the ring was deafening as Mike and I lay still in bed knowing this call was not simply an interruption to our quiet little house but more of an uprooting of our quiet little family.

With a few contemplative moments and a quick prayer, we answered the call with a yes to a caseworker asking us to care for a two-month-old little boy. I want to be careful to protect this little boy and his big story, but just know there's so much I could write that is mind-blowing, heartbreaking, and God exalting through the process. I could literally go on for days about God's goodness in the hardest places we faced in the coming months.

But let me just net it out here by summing up our entire foster care journey with this statement:

> *We went into the foster care journey scared of what it might do to our family; we came out of it scared of who we would be if we had not done it.*

And that's just how God works—He calls us into the most ridiculously hard places that we wouldn't dare walk on our own because we feel completely inadequate and unqualified. Not to mention we're perfectly content in the margins of our own status quo lives.

But then there's God—who, right there in the middle of the impossible, asks us to participate in things we've previously only read about in the Bible. We see how He's faithfully giving the vulnerable a voice and prioritizing the marginalized. And in doing this, we're offered a small part in kingdom-building, eternally significant work simply by giving our most reluctant *yes*. Only God.

THE *Right* THING IS RARELY THE *Easy* THING

A few hours after that middle-of-the-night phone call, we found ourselves holding a precious little baby dropped off with little more than a half-empty bottle and a single diaper. Mike was walking in from the store with supplies when our kids came downstairs to the cries of a new baby. They were armed with a plethora of questions we really couldn't answer:

> *What's his story?*
> *Where is his mom?*
> *Why couldn't she care for a baby?*
> *How long is he staying with us?*
> *Aren't you too old to take care of a newborn baby?* (On
> second thought, this particular question was my
> own.)

Even with no concrete answers to give at the time, we wanted our kids to understand one very important thing about this baby's story: his mama made a brave decision by carrying out this pregnancy. This baby represents a sacrificial love that likely included nine months of hushed conversations, humiliating circumstances, and harsh criticism. Pregnant teenagers don't often have baby showers and Meal Trains with friends standing by to celebrate a new addition to life. Nonetheless, she stayed the course, demonstrating how doing the right thing is rarely the easy thing—but it's still right.

In the days that followed, I often wondered how many times that mama looked into her baby's sweet, dark eyes, questioning how she could possibly persevere with no experience, minimal resources, and a limited support system to care for a baby. And then as weeks turned into months, I found myself looking into those same sweet, dark eyes, questioning how our family would possibly weather this journey with no set timetable and the impossible task of protecting our hearts as we grew increasingly attached to him.

It was crushing to navigate the court-appointed visitations and see his biological family work through the difficult process. Yet I was also wrecked at the reality that this little boy might be moved to a place where his safety and well-being were uncertain.

Our kids left for school many days not knowing if he would be there when they got home. And on those same days, I would find myself in the afternoon carpool surrounded by a crew of kids desperate to know if he was still in my backseat. I'm blown away by the people who had no vote in our foster care decision yet completely invested in and loved this little boy as their own.

Time after time, our community bought diapers, held bottles, and prayed relentlessly when we couldn't possibly do it on our own. And on one particularly hard day in a very raw conversation, a friend asked if we would do foster care again if this little boy was taken from our home. I responded vulnerably and honestly saying, "I don't know if I can do it again. It's really, really hard."

But our nine-year-old son, overhearing the conversation, jumped right in saying, *"But Mom, just because it's hard doesn't mean it's not right."* And I instantly knew that my son—much like this baby's teenage mom—understood that doing the right thing is rarely the easy thing, but we do it anyway.

We're far from saints but just normal people who took the off-ramp from our exhausting first-world life in hopes of pursuing something bigger than ourselves.

LOVING WHAT GOD LOVES

Just under two years into our foster care journey, against all odds, a court ruled in favor of this little boy staying with us. We adopted him shortly thereafter, surrounded by the many, many people who held our arms up like Aaron and Hur held Moses's when he was too weak to do it on his own (Ex. 17:12). And even in the midst of our own celebration, we mourned the hardship and pain that will always mark this journey for our son, his biological mother, and all those who walked the very broken road with us.

We changed his name to Joshua, the English version of his given name, Josué. He goes by his initials, JB (Joshua Bo), which perfectly suits this outgoing little boy who has never met a stranger. Incidentally, Joshua is Hebrew for "God is salvation" or "God saves." And while I'm guessing his biological mother didn't know the significance of that name when she picked it for this little boy, rest assured it is not lost on us.

Truly, God *is* salvation. JB's story points to the larger story of a God who longs to save us from our most dire places and adopt us into His family for all eternity. He pursues us—don't miss that. He literally chases after us because He loves us and wants us to trust Him with our lives, even if the best we have to offer in return is a reluctant yes.

Once in a while, when I share JB's story, someone will remark that we've earned a jewel in our crown or we're saints because of this journey. I assume it's because I'll be navigating kindergarten and menopause all at the same time. But truly, our story isn't unusual by God's standards—calling a believer to take care of orphans and love people, well—that's not exceptional or extraordinary … it's just biblical.

That's the thing about loving what God loves. He cares deeply about many of the things we would prefer to sweep under the rug.

He loves the homeless, the panhandlers, the drug addicted, and the dealers. He's burdened by the hurts in the parts of town we've been avoiding, and He's restoring the stories we've become comfortable overlooking.

What used to be a statistic now has a face and a name in our family. And we're far from saints but just normal people who took the off-ramp from our exhausting, first-world life in hopes of pursuing something bigger than ourselves. I've since realized I spent way too many years living in the margins of my faith and playing it safe, and I'm now challenged to love the things of God even when everything in me wants to love the things of this world.

I think our daughter, Kate, best summarized our foster care journey in these words as a part of her college application essay:

> Trash bags. It was impossible to look past the trash bags as I waited in the cold, unwelcoming Child Protective Services office. These bags may have only held a few treasured possessions, but they were overflowing with emotional baggage. I watched in curiosity as I saw young children rush in and out of the doors. Some waited for a parent who would never show up. Some nervously awaited placement in yet another foster home. How could these innocent children be placed in such difficult situations through no fault of their own? Here I was in a part of town that I had never been before, in a world I could never imagine existed, learning a lesson I'll never forget. Those trash bags represented real

children with hard stories, and behind every trash bag was an opportunity to help someone.

Six-hundred and twenty-three days. That is how long my family fostered this little boy before adopting him. This time was marked by many ups, as well as many downs. There were days I spent hours upon hours playing with that precious little boy. There were other days when I went to school not knowing if he would still be at our house when I came home. I learned that the process of foster care is marked by uncertainty. But in the uncertainty of whether the baby stayed with us, I learned that tomorrow's uncertainty should drive what we choose to do today. We must love well today, meet needs today, and make the most of opportunities today. Knowing this taught me the importance of living in the moment and using what limited time we are given to make a difference and help others today.

Trash bags and living for today marked my experience with foster care and an overall change in my way of thinking. I used to run from life's messy trash bags that could cause me hardships; now I look for them as opportunities to help others. I used to see time as a resource to simply accomplish my own goals; now I see each day as a once-in-a-lifetime opportunity to serve others and to live bigger than myself. People always tell me that adoption changed my little brother's life. But the truth is, it changed mine.

It's true, we went into this foster care journey scared of what it might do to our family. But we came out of it scared of who we would be if we had not done it. We are changed people. We've seen how—even during those long, quiet nights of lying next to JB's crib and crying out to the Lord to do His very best for this little boy—God was present and faithful to hear our prayers while also changing our hearts to more closely resemble His.

And just as our family will never be able to unsee the rooms full of children holding all their possessions in trash bags while waiting on a parent who may not show up, the Lord can't unsee the struggles around us every day.

The Lord has authored a new prayer in our lives. A prayer that our days will be spent willing to take risks that don't add up, refusing to live another day calculating the cost, and stepping into other people's stories because that's how we love what God loves.

CHAPTER 4

The Fine Print of Friendship

MESSY TRUTH

If Jesus healed a paralytic because of the faith of
his friends, you can be assured your circle matters.

*I*was at a birthday lunch with some of my closest friends when I felt a strange thud in my heart. A wave of nausea hit me, and I suddenly felt light-headed, as if I might pass out. Having consulted Google for every ache and pain in the last twenty years, I began to worry about a heart attack (or cancer, always cancer). So I anxiously described my symptoms to my friends.

As expected, they all jumped into action and reached for their purses. I naively assumed they were reaching for their phones to call an ambulance, because normal people understand that time is critical when you're dealing with potentially life-threatening health issues.

But these girls are far from normal, and they came out of those purses armed with an arsenal of essential oils. Yes, *essential oils*. I kid you not, they had the lavender and lemongrass flowing before I knew what hit me. They were spraying wrists and dabbing earlobes while simultaneously debating the merits of peppermint over chamomile given my current symptoms.

Thankfully, I began to feel better as I waited for Ashton Kutcher to jump out.

Since neither Ashton nor an ambulance showed up that day, I spent the next few minutes trying to explain to these lovely women that in the case of an actual emergency, one would prefer a hospital over hyssop. That defibrillators and doctors are more effective than essential oils in scenarios where one might need an EKG and some paddles.

It didn't resonate. They still claim a miraculous essential-oil healing that day that defied traditional medicine (and common sense too, I might add).

MATTERS OF THE HEART

But goodness, I love these girls.

We refer to ourselves as the Wednesday Lunchers because we've been having lunch every week for the last fifteen-plus years.

We met in a neighborhood that most of us have long since moved away from. And with small kids back in the day, we spent lots of time at the neighborhood pool, the nasty bounce house places, and virtually any other kid-friendly location that could accommodate the five of us with sixteen kids in tow. (We were also big fans of the gym cafe because there's childcare available while you pretend to be working out. Win. Win.)

We have always been resolute in our weekly Chick-fil-A lunches because who doesn't need a good dose of God's chicken, Diet Coke, and a playground for the kids? And now that the majority of our kids have outgrown the playground tubes and weekly lunches with Mom, we've relocated to a local grocery store with a convenient little eatery attached.

My heart scare all those years ago at lunch only scratches the surface of heart issues we've weathered together as friends. We've faced divorce, death, and defiant children. We've walked through anxiety attacks, adoptions, lost jobs, and even a devastating affair. We've lost parents to cancer, sent kids to college, prayed for a kidney donor, and even as I write these words, we're waiting for a few prodigals to make their way home.

We could teach a class on the perils of raising kids, discipline, learning differences, kids' friendships, dating relationships, technology use, and sports. And even though our kids now range in ages from twenty down to six, we're still parenting them with everything we've got, which sometimes feels like it's not quite enough.

These girls are tried and true. They are real, compassionate, and ridiculously funny. They know no boundaries—and frankly, they really should learn some when it comes to sharing about things like hormone pellets and colonoscopies.

We know each other well enough to finish each other's sentences, yet we listen intently because the time around the table each Wednesday is significant. Sure, there are plenty of weeks that are forgettable and unnoteworthy, but there are just as many that are hard and meaningful and leave us crying in the middle of a grocery store because, when one of us hurts, we never hurt alone.

What I probably love the most about these particular friends is that, even when everything seems to be crumbling around us, we are guaranteed that, for at least a few hours each Wednesday, we will be seen, heard, and loved no matter what we bring to the table.

I believe friendships are one of the Lord's sweetest gifts—those true friends who know your deepest flaws but love you anyway. I've experienced it in the girls I'm talking about here as well as many other precious friendships that are scattered throughout the chapters of this book. I joke with my friends that I'm the Taylor Swift of book writing—you wrong me and I'll publish it to memorialize forever. But thankfully, the pages would be virtually blank if I ever set out to write that book.

Real, deep friendships always remind me of one of my favorite felt-board Bible stories. Surely you've experienced the Sunday school felt-board stories back in the day? The pale blue background where you put a tiny Zacchaeus in the big tree because he's too short to see Jesus teaching below? Or Noah loading his felt ark whereby you and a friend, two by two of course, are called up to the easel to place the animals on the boat ramp?

Well, my personal favorite felt-board Bible story is about a guy who was paralyzed and spent his days lying on a mat (Luke 5:17–26). He had four amazing friends who understood that nothing short of a miracle was going to heal him, so they jumped into action and grabbed their essential oils. Thankfully, not.

They heard Jesus was in town, and they knew He was their friend's only hope. So they picked up the very mat where he lay and hauled him to the house where Jesus was teaching. But the crowds were great that day, and his friends couldn't even make it to the front door, much less to Jesus.

Yet these guys weren't easily dissuaded, and they knew that when a door closes, a window opens—or maybe a roof.

They made their way up to the roof (dragging their paralyzed friend along with them) and began digging a hole. They dug and dug until the hole was large enough to fit their friend and his mat through it. Then they lowered him down and waited for Jesus to do what only He could do for their friend.

Seriously, picture this for a minute.

These four guys literally raised the roof in the name of friendship, lowering their paralyzed friend down from the ceiling, all while interrupting Jesus' teaching in a room full of religious elites.

That story preaches.

Jesus, seeing the faith of the man's friends, healed the man spiritually first and physically second. And what started with four crazy friends and a harebrained idea ended with a paralyzed man picking up his mat and walking away in complete freedom.

THE POWER OF FOUR

I wonder, in a culture that tells us we need perfect kids, the right zip code, a big bank account, and the perfect social media feed, if we could dare believe that all we really need is just four crazy friends and Jesus?

Because four friends who understand the fine print of friendships will show up and do the very things we can't do on our own. They will refuse to go one more day watching us feel pitied, passed by, overlooked, and ostracized. They are compassionate and kind but also willful and spirited.

It's not just any four friends who get the job done, though, because the wrong four friends turn around and go home when the front door is crowded. The wrong four don't see a solution beyond the problem. The wrong four are worried about what people are going to think. The wrong four don't see past their own problems. The wrong four assume someone else will get the job done. The wrong four give up hope.

But the right four—oh, those are the ones who will make it happen.

> The right four never stop dreaming your dreams.
> The right four won't stop fighting for your marriage.
> The right four don't lose faith in your recovery.
> The right four don't give up on your kids.

The right four won't stop short of dragging your chubby butt to higher ground because they know God's got more for you than the mess you're sitting in at that moment.

But it also takes a little humility along the way. The paralytic didn't refuse his friends' help because it was too much to ask, or he needed more privacy, or he had a reputation to protect. Nope, he was well aware of his dire state and darn sure wasn't going to allow his pride to push away the people who loved him the very most.

If Jesus healed the paralytic in large part because of the faith of his friends, you can be assured that your circle matters. Finding your four matters. Or maybe it's five, or three, or one, or however many friends the Lord calls into your life and calls you to be in theirs.

But by all means, don't miss the most critical component of the four—they always point you to the One.

Jesus is the only one who heals our hearts first because He cares even more about our spiritual paralyses than our physical ones. He's the only one who brings quiet to the chaos. He's the only one who knows the very hardest thing you're facing at this exact moment and will bring you peace if you'll lean in and trust Him in the unknown.

HYSSOP AND THE HEART OF FRIENDSHIP

I've found that friendships are so often our most valuable lifelines when life gets hard and we've somehow lost our way. But I've also learned that it doesn't happen by settling for anything less than the real thing. Scrolling social media feeds or binging Netflix shows has never created a deep community. Pretending everything is perfect,

The fine print of friendships has taught me to make time when there's barely any to be spared. To show up with the most authentic and vulnerable version of myself when it's easier to say everything's fine.

or hanging on to a crowd that's never going to fully accept you, is a soul crusher for next-level friendships.

The fine print of friendships has taught me to make time when there's barely any to be spared. To show up with the most authentic and vulnerable version of myself when it's easier to say everything's fine. It's listening instead of speaking and going light on judgment and heavy on compassion because there're many roads we'll never walk.

I chuckled recently when I ran across references to hyssop in the Bible. I started thinking about my friends at lunch during my purported heart attack and the mishap with the essential oils. Apparently hyssop was used in biblical times for those suffering with health problems such as leprosy, and even (brace yourselves) chest ailments. So even though I'll never admit it to my girls, I guess a little bit of hyssop wasn't all that far off after all.

There's an anonymous quote floating around that summarizes the fine print of friendship perfectly. It says, "Show me your friends, and I'll show you your future."

Yes, how blessed we are if we have determined, purposeful, decisive, persevering, crazy, and godly friends who leave no (wo)man behind—not only today but for whatever life throws our way.

CHAPTER 5

Believing Forward

MESSY TRUTH

Today is the perfect day to stop worrying about what the world says good parents are supposed to do and instead do what we're called to do.

I can't pinpoint the first time I remember *really* wanting to have kids. I just always seemed to know I wanted to be a mom. Some of my earliest childhood memories are the days I spent feeding my dolls their bottles while dog-earing the pages of the Sears catalog with car seats, swings, clothes, and all the essentials I would need should I suddenly (and inexplicably) have a real baby of my own.

My mom was a saint, and knowing how much I loved babies, she set up baby playdates for me. Like, she literally called ladies in the church with little ones and asked if we could babysit them so I could play with their babies. Today this might land me with a background check and an entry-level package of counseling sessions, but for my eight-year-old self it was a little slice of heaven.

My mom had this unique gift of allowing me to believe forward in the things of the future by giving me glimpses of it in the moment.

And so here I was, a little girl dying to have a baby someday, with my mom arranging playdates for her baby to play with someone else's. And it was loads of fun—for *me* anyway. (On a similar note, when my middle-school brothers wanted to be truck drivers, Dorothy took them to every truck yard within a sixty-mile-radius so they could dream their best Peterbilt dreams. There are no words for sweet Dorothy.)

NURSERIES AND MOWING

Having always loved me a good baby, you can imagine how excited I was in my late twenties to find out Mike and I were expecting our first child. It's quite the miracle that I even figured out how to have a baby after Dorothy gave the vaguest "birds and bees" talk you've ever heard. It left my junior-high self convinced that the "condiments on request" sign at McDonald's was a ploy to put birth control in Happy Meals. And now my kids claim I've passed down that same vague "birds and the bees" talk to them, and I have no plans to remedy it.

Nonetheless, I immediately harnessed every little bit of my baby-crazed past and began creating a nursery that was altogether breathtaking (yet also somewhat embarrassing as I consider it in hindsight). Don't judge me for Kate's over-the-top nursery, because you've done a few of those same "first child" things too, and I'm willing to dig out your Creative Memories scrapbooks to prove it.

It wasn't just the mural above her four-poster crib that was a bit much, but something about the combination of her custom bedding, the hand-painted rocking chair, the chandelier, the monogrammed blankets, the board books, the Baby Einstein mobile, the color-coordinated stuffed animals, and the dresses upon dresses that made her nursery extraordinary. It was a couple hundred square feet of baby fabulousness, and nothing was going to take that away from me Kate.

That was until a few months into her little life when I realized that her days and nights were mixed up, and in my sleep-deprived frenzy I ripped the same custom bedding and brainy mobile right out of her crib like a deranged lunatic. I feel sure that some expert in a *Babywise* chat room (did we even have those back then?) told me that bumper pads and crib mobiles might "overstimulate" one's baby, thereby causing said child to stay awake in their crib crying night after night after night after night.

It was around this same time that my husband realized I might be suffering from a mild case of the postpartum depressions. In fact, the whole neighborhood was surely aware of it once I convinced my reluctant husband to let me mow the yard each week. It was a pitiful sight—me out there on Lochwood Drive mowing meticulous lines back and forth while crying big tears and contemplating how anyone survives a newborn.

I'm altogether unclear as to why I insisted on mowing the grass in that season, but somehow working in our little yard was therapeutic for a girl on maternity leave from her law job and in desperate need of a win.

The postpartum drama was especially pronounced one unremarkable Saturday morning when Kate was fussy. I had the sudden realization I had to get away from that baby—and fast. I remember briskly standing up and handing our precious baby over to my husband, saying in my most resolute voice, "I (insert pregnant pause) am going to Hobby Lobby."

I mean, some people in desperate places freak out and skip town or go to a bar or meet up with an old fling. I apparently go to the local arts and crafts store. (I heart you, Hobby Lobby!) I cried up and down the aisles of Christmas trees and ornaments that June day, and a sweet woman gave me a hug and told me it was going to be okay. And after a few months more, it was.

I've loved being a mom ever since, or at least on more days than not.

THE MIDDLE FINGER AND THE READING CLUB

By the time our second child, Brett, came along, I was pretty sure I had the parenting thing all figured out since, you know, I'd been a mom for like three years or something. Interestingly enough, I've found the teeniest bit of parenting experience, coupled with a moderately compliant firstborn, brings out a mom's very most inner-sanctimoniousness. I recently heard someone say young moms write how-to books on parenting while older moms write how-to books on prayer.

I must have been in the thick of my how-to parenting book when Brett hit first grade and God had some work to do in me. I had just finished leading a prayer meeting for the moms at our school when I saw the voicemail from his first grade teacher. I returned the call only to learn Brett had been real busy flipping off his colleagues before school that morning.

According to Noah (still one of his closest friends to this day), Brett flipped off everyone and everything in the cafeteria, including the ceiling ... which Noah translated as flipping off Jesus. And since flipping off Jesus is *no bueno* in a small private Christian school, Brett and I got a talkin' to. That's when I began writing how-to prayer books.

A few months later I received another call from the school, this time letting me know that Brett was falling behind in reading. They were putting him in the reading club, which was one of the few "clubs" at our new school we had hoped not to join. Essentially, it's a great program for kids who need an extra boost in reading; however, it also means you're not reading at grade level and are in need of said boost.

Naturally, I interpreted the teacher's phone call as the beginning of the end and went straight down a path of insanity like this: Since he isn't successful in first grade, there's no way he can make it through elementary school. And with no basics under his belt, he won't finish high school and definitely not college. There's no hope for future job opportunities and so the best we can do at this point is just make him comfortable.

I know, right?

So a few short hours later, I found myself driving tearfully to school to pick up Brett, wondering how I was possibly going to relay the tragic news to him. I was sure this day marked the beginning of Brett being set apart from his peers, labeled, and treated as not good enough because he struggled academically.

Now, sweet Brett, unaware of all my internal crazy, bounced right out of that school, and before the car door even closed, he declared, "It was the best day ever, Mom! I got picked for the reading club!"

Let's agree to disagree, kid.

It seems his teacher had quite reasonably explained the reading club model to him while also mentioning he had several friends joining him for this great adventure. Brett was thrilled to have been "picked," and aren't we thankful his teacher got to him before I did?

WHAT GOOD MOMS ARE SUPPOSED TO DO

There's really no substitute for the gift of time and perspective. Brett is now in high school, and I'm grateful for a broader lens as I look back. Although, thankfully, Brett reads fine now, those early reading club days marked the beginning of some tough roads we walked with Brett academically.

My struggle was always in the messaging and not the messenger, hearing words that seemed to imply my son was different or broken or not good enough.

Of course, that's not at all what anyone was saying—but that's what I heard, and I couldn't stand the thought of him lacking anything in any way. I would have gone to any lengths to shield him from this because I thought that's what good moms were supposed to do.

I realize now Brett *was* in fact being broken down. Just not in the ways I had feared. Just as fire is used to purify gold, the Lord began to so graciously use Brett's struggles to take away the impurities of self-sufficiency, arrogance, and pride while replacing them with hard work, empathy, and kindness.

Today is the day to pray your most ridiculous parenting prayers and wait with dogged anticipation for HIS answers.

All my fears of Brett being labeled, set apart, and feeling inadequate faded as I began to see him labeled … with kindness. Or set apart … for his faith. And learning that he's truly not good enough … but he can trust in the One who is.

And you know what really gets me?

In my most well-intentioned yet fearful moments, I would have robbed Brett of all that God was doing because it wasn't a part of my plan. I couldn't yet see the nose-to-the-grindstone work ethic God was creating in him that would later impact not only Brett's academics but also his friendships, athletics, faith, and drive to succeed. *The very path I had so desperately hoped to shield Brett from has been our most tangible evidence of God working in and through his life.*

Parenting has repeatedly taught me that you don't know what you don't know. But thankfully, God does. And just as my mom was teaching me to believe forward in what God could do all those years ago through something as simple as holding someone else's child, God has been teaching me to believe forward in my very hardest places of parenting while lovingly holding me as His precious child.

That's just who God is. He's the one who

In your most mind-blowing, soul-crushing, agenda-interrupting parts of life, promises to work all things for your good and His glory

Brings beauty from the ashes of your struggling marriage, financial missteps, friendship losses, and health scares

Is trustworthy even when life goes off script and
all your parenting dreams seem to be slipping
through your fingers

Calms the storms and moves the mountains all
while using today's struggles for tomorrow's
sanctification

Asks us to lay off the mom judgment and walk hard
roads with those simply trying to figure it out
like we all are

Brings eternal significance to your deepest parenting struggles if only you will believe forward in
His greater plan for your family

Today is the day to pray your most ridiculous parenting prayers
and wait with dogged anticipation for His answers. It's the day
to gather your Ebenezers—the reminders of where God's been so
faithful in the past—and declare with every ounce of grit and deter-
mination that you will trust Him today.

Today is the day to stop worrying about what "good moms are
supposed to do" and live as a godly mom who knows what she's
called to do.

And as we wait together patiently, believing forward in a God
who works in the hardest places of parenting, follow my mom's lead
and go hold someone else's baby or kick the tires at the eighteen-
wheeler lot or rejoice in the reading club while you trust that God's
got this.

CHAPTER 6

When Church Hurts

MESSY TRUTH

There may be a million reasons to walk away from the church, but Jesus is the one reason to stay.

*C*hurch people are funny.

I can say this because I was born and raised in the church, so I'm well versed in church people and love every one of their idiosyncrasies. If an expert is defined as someone with a comprehensive knowledge of a subject, then Serena Williams is an expert on tennis, Kim Kardashian on self-promotion, and me on church people.

CHURCH-SPEAK

One of the funny things about church people is they say things that only make sense to other churchgoers, with zero self-awareness that such things might be perceived as strange. It reminds me of a high-school friend whose parents openly passed gas in their home without skipping a beat. Somewhere along the way it had become commonplace to freely flatulate, and they lost sight of the fact that outsiders might find this behavior off-putting.

You can imagine a dozen teens hanging out for a movie night when Mom casually breaks wind while refilling the popcorn bowl— well, there ain't a thirteen-year-old in the world mature enough to overlook it. Our initial reaction was, *Oh, how embarrassing; it must have slipped*, until we realized Dad and Brother were also free-spirited flatulators. So when in Rome … Just kidding.

My husband didn't grow up in church, so he really gets a kick out of our church protocols. And since we're also talking toots, one time he accidentally passed gas in a youth group prayer time. Being horrified, he made the next right move by putting on his best shocked face and staring in disgust at the guy sitting directly next to him.

But the problem with church talk and openly passing gas is that they both have the potential of getting a little bit weird and a whole lot stinky.

We church people have been known to pray a "hedge of protection" over a prayer request, assuming shrubbery is the answer to one's direst of needs. When someone says something ironic, we respond with our most robust "amen." We speak a completely different language, especially on Sundays, when some of the more formal of us call the program a "bulletin" and refer to the sit-down-and-shut-up music as a "prelude."

You undoubtedly get what I'm saying, and that's probably plenty of examples of church talk, but I'm on a roll now and can't stop—so I won't.

When a potential new minister preaches, it's called "in view of a call." If someone is going to share the gospel in a scary place, we jump on out there and "commission" him before sending him off for his potentially ill-fated journey. Having a new baby means an addition to the "cradle roll," and we enjoy a good acronym like GAs (Girls in Action), RAs (Royal Ambassadors), and VBS (vacation Bible school).

We church people also love us a good committee, so much so that we have a group called the "committee on committees" whose sole job is to slate the rest of the committees. And then there's dropping off the poinsettias to the people we call "shut-ins" (those who can't get to church). Never mind they wouldn't be "shut-in" if we would pick them up and take them to church—but sorry, no time because I got me a committee meeting.

Let's not limit our preciousness to the things we *say* at church, because there're plenty of unusual things we actually *do*. We take "love offerings" when there's a missionary visiting, and we hold hands with strangers across the aisle when wrapping up a casual Sunday evening service.

We play handbells with embarrassing vigor, and I particularly like how we sometimes ask those who have accepted Jesus to quietly raise their hands while everyone else *promises* to keep their eyes shut. I mean, would it be so horrifying to publicly acknowledge you've come to faith in Jesus in a church, of all places? We're super considerate that way, except that a few weeks later we will baptize you in an ill-fitting church T-shirt surrounded by a room full of people who are suddenly bound and determined to keep their eyes open lest they be accused of sleeping. Eyes open, eyes closed—it's anyone's guess on the right protocol.

We have ice cream socials, lock-in retreats for kids, and in the old days we even enjoyed Tuesday night visitation. To clarify, visitation entails passing out the previous Sunday's visitor slips and then driving to that particular "prospect's" home and knocking on their door. As if it's not awkward enough visiting a church and not knowing anyone in the building, we march it right up to your homestead and invite ourselves in to tell you why you can't afford to miss the fun things we're doing.

THINGS YOU LEARN AT CHURCH

We also do holidays real special as church people, especially Christmas because it's *our* holiday, evidenced by the name. I grew up in a church that had a Christmas spectacular each year called the Living Singing Christmas Tree. I'm sorry if you've missed this particular event, but I'll do my best to unpack it (another great church word).

The *men* of the church (I know) would get together on Sunday after a potluck lunch and pull out a ginormous wooden structure to be erected into a large platform in the shape of a Christmas tree: picture bleachers three stories high with stairs going up one side. The *ladies* (yes, I still know) then followed up a few days later with garland and lights and decorated the structure to look like a Christmas tree (kinda like what Jesus had) so the choir could stand on it and perform.

Now, each year a senior in high school was picked to be the top of the tree. It was quite the honor because it included a solo and a pretty high likelihood of passing out. Yes, routinely someone on the tree either passed out or puked from the heat, and the only way down required all the people on the levels below to exit first. You quickly learned to gird your loins (and your hair) from a host of things that might be coming your way from on high. I say all of this in jest, but I truly loved this performance each year.

Oh, and thanks for asking! Yes, I was asked to be at the top of the tree my senior year. I declined based on a fairly established issue with claustrophobia and a budding fear of heights. But I did get a solo and didn't pass out or puke, so overall it was a win. Nevertheless, people came from far and wide to see this show, and to this day the memories pour back anytime I smell singed garland, vomit, or hear the "Hallelujah" chorus.

Now, as much as I laugh at the funny things of the church, I can also say with utmost sincerity that my most treasured memories and formative beliefs about God have come from the precious people in the church. Church people have taught me God is present in the unwanted testimonies of loss and suffering. That generosity is not a matter of finances but of faith. They have challenged me to do hard things and cautioned me when I've made things about me that were never mine to claim.

I've seen my parents do life with other Christians and experienced firsthand a community raising me up to love God and do what's right.

I've watched church people experience unfathomable hardships while simultaneously holding fast to a God who gives and takes away.

I've been taught that earth is not my home, so I can hold my today loosely knowing my tomorrow is secure.

I've sung the same hymns as Christians hundreds of years before me and literally cried at the words of "It Is Well with My Soul":

> *And Lord, haste the day when my faith shall be sight*
> *The clouds be rolled back as a scroll*
> *The trump shall resound, and the Lord shall descend*
> *Even so, it is well with my soul!*[1]

THAT'S GONNA LEAVE A MARK

Yet I would be remiss if I didn't also say some of my biggest emotional hurts in the last decade have come from people in the church. People who love Jesus and get it right more often than not have devastated me with their actions, their words, and their complicity. I've felt overlooked, misunderstood, minimized, and dismissed.

We've shared weddings, the birth of babies, the loss of family, and the hardest places life throws our way, only making it that much more excruciating when they hurt me or those I love. I now understand why some say church hurts are the deepest hurts—because it's the very people with whom you are most vulnerable, share mission, and will spend eternity who seem to have dealt some of the most painful blows.

Even so, the people in the church are my people.

They will get it wrong, as will I, but they will still be my most treasured family. I find comfort knowing Jesus created the church for the broken, the misguided, the imperfect, and the imposters. Seems I, too, vacillate between most of those roles any given day.

I'm reminded that Jesus called the church His bride, His body, and the place where He quite literally dwells. It's the God-ordained establishment for those desperately seeking refreshment that comes only from the living water. We come empty yet leave full when we gather before the One to whom all glory, praise, and honor is due.

It's critical to remember that church people aren't God. God is God. And we get into dangerous territory when we start confusing this distinction.

There's a critical thing to remember—church people aren't God. God is God. And we get into dangerous territory when we start confusing this very important distinction by allowing the missteps of humans to inform our beliefs about God.

I've figured out my church hurts really aren't from the church at all. My hurts have come from flawed individuals who are often the loudest voices in the room. Yet I'm reminded it's the still, small voice that carries the only true significance, and He is good, just, forgiving, and unchanging. No person can deal a finishing blow because Jesus already took it on my behalf.

To miss the beauty of church because of the missteps of its people is tempting but also short-sighted. If our country was at war and I had the opportunity to go to the White House each week to talk with the president, learn of our readiness, get clarity on his battle plan, and walk the very halls where he resides, would I turn down this opportunity because someone in the gatehouse offended me? Would I walk away from the undeserved knowledge, power, and shelter I've been offered simply because of the music in the lunchroom?

Our culture is at war, and Christian values are being attacked like never before. We can't afford to let the flawed fragments of the church destroy our very greatest ammunition of gathering and supporting each other in pursuit of Jesus. Our culture cannot afford for us to be distracted and divided by things with no eternal bearing when our call is to make His name known.

Yet the enemy would love nothing more. *He wins when we withdraw.*

So I'll summarize church like this:

If you're looking for people who talk weird, go to
church.

If you're looking for people who sometimes do
strange things, go to church.

If you're looking for hypocrisy and brokenness, go
to church.

If you're looking for glimpses of dogma and division, go to church.

But also,

If you're looking for healing and rest, go to church.

If you're looking for mission and renewed purpose,
go to church.

If you're looking for people who will walk with you
in the deepest struggles, go to church.

If you're looking for a casserole topped with corn-
flakes after your next surgery, go to church.

And by all means, if you're looking for the people of God, go
to church.

At this very moment, I'm sitting in a church writing these
words. It's not a church I attend, but one that's close to my home
with a covered patio overlooking a small pond and a huge white
cross. I find when things are heavy or uncertain or when I need the
Lord to give me a word as I'm speaking into something that seems
impossibly hard … it's best found in the church.

I'm genuinely sorry for the hurt so many of us have experienced from church people. I hate that some days I still fight the temptation to resent the people who hurt me so deeply. I feel like over the years I've had a million reasons to walk away. But even so—as I sit here watching happy and friendly people pass by—I'm at peace, even if for just a moment in this church, knowing Jesus is my one reason to stay.

CHAPTER 7

What Nobody Tells You

MESSY TRUTH

We mistakenly believe the mishaps, annoyances,
and character-building moments are life's small
things, not realizing they are actually the big
things crafting the very DNA of our family.

*I*t was a few weeks before Christmas, and I decided it was time to debunk the whole Santa thing with Kate. It's admittedly controversial to spill the beans to an otherwise fully believing kid, but it was time.

Let's be clear: this was in no way a spiritual decision. I wasn't afraid that Santa being pretend would translate to Jesus being pretend, dashing her chances of a faith-filled life. I'm also not one of those people who only buys three Christmas gifts for our kids because that's all Jesus had. I mean, Jesus was born in a stable and you people are still using hospitals, so there's that.

But the girl was literally halfway through sixth grade, and she still had no clue. It was getting embarrassing. We would take her little brother for Santa pics, and Kate would come armed with her own detailed list for Santa. In CURSIVE. She watched the Santa Tracker religiously each Christmas Eve, naming the continents as he passed.

I felt sure someone at school was going to pants her if she kept up this whole Santa routine, so I finally broke it down one afternoon and let the cat out of the bag. She took it harder than I anticipated, asking if she could take the car for a drive as she worked things out by herself.

With that big revelation behind me, I jumped in the shower before heading out for the evening. But like clockwork, Kate came knocking on the bathroom door every five minutes or so, as the gravity of this new information set in. *Knock, knock, knock.* "Easter bunny?" Yes, Kate, the Easter bunny is also pretend.

Five minutes later. *Knock, knock, knock.* "Tooth fairy?" Yes, sweetie, the tooth fairy is also pretend. Five minutes later. *Knock,*

knock, knock. "Elf on the Shelf?" Now it's become sheer melodrama, because everyone knows we're not good enough parents to move an elf around each night from sitting on toilets to sipping through drinking straws in dog bowls.

Eventually, after she finished setting up her counseling appointments, Kate very purposefully came in with one last question: "So is every parent in on this?" *Yes, Kate, all parents know about this.*

She turned and walked out of my room in her most indignant manner, mumbling, "Why didn't anyone tell me?"

I totally relate to that sentiment because it's basically the story of my life. Believing in things that nobody told me about, only to later realize everyone else was in on it. It's not the big, life-changing, earth-shattering things. No, it's just the dumb stuff everyone seems to have figured out somewhere or somehow along the way. So as your friend and someone who tends to be the last to know, here's what nobody tells you about marriage, parenting, and traveling with small kids.

You're welcome.

ABOUT MARRIAGE

Mike and I had our first "real" fight just a few months before our wedding. We met at Sonic for lunch because we're fancy that way, and to say I was armed and ready for a throwdown would be an understatement. And to say Mike was completely blindsided while downing his Chili Cheese Coney Combo would also be an understatement.

Let's blame it on the millions of itty-bitty tiny things to be done before the wedding day (because otherwise the nuptials don't count) that sent me over the edge. Or maybe it's just the whole thing of spending your entire childhood dreaming of your wedding day so there ain't nothing or nobody going to screw it up—not even Mr. Right.

It was a few weeks before the Sonic scandal when I asked my sweet fiancé to help me put together a playlist for our rehearsal dinner. At the time, we had a family band (it's not as bad as it sounds) who agreed to play some after-dinner music, which Mike happily agreed to coordinate.

Why, you ask, did I think this particular playlist needed coordinating? I have no idea and that's on me.

But surely you can appreciate that coordinating a playlist is one of those things we (women) can knock out in about two seconds while also holding a baby on the hip, throwing dinner in the crockpot, and firing off an email to the PTA president declining to chair the spring fundraiser.

My sweet fiancé, on the other hand, was not quite as efficient in his duties and got obsessed with which songs to play. He spent weeks on gut-wrenching choices like "Every Rose Has Its Thorn" (yes, he really picked that song) or "Sister Golden Hair" in the first set. Naturally, I'd had it this day at Sonic and informed Mike of my need for him to pick up the pace and get back to the more critical things of our wedding like table confetti, birdseed sachets, and personalized disposable cameras (please tell me you had those on every table like we did).

Turns out the joke was on me.

Playlists do in fact matter, and my failure to focus on our reception music (as Mike did so "thoroughly" for the rehearsal dinner music) resulted in our live band playing "Sexual Healing" smack-dab in the middle of our straitlaced, alcohol-free, Baptist-inundated reception. All the planning in the world can't make you unsee Mike and me awkwardly dancing to "I'm hot just like an oven, I need some lovin'."[1]

Just as nobody told me our precious husbands sometimes obsess over seemingly meaningless things that end up mattering more than we think, there's a multitude of other things about marriage (and mainly husbands) nobody tells you that go something like this:

- An offer to help you get ready for a dinner party might include organizing the back of his truck after checking all the batteries in the smoke detectors.
- His version of consoling you after a tough day looks nothing like your version of consolation.
- Remembering your mother's birthday is outside of his memory capacity but he knows offhand who won the 1985 World Series (Kansas City Royals) and the year Sammy Hagar left Van Halen (1996).
- He truly doesn't notice the empty toilet paper roll, yet his prepper tendencies have the hall closet filled with months of shelf-stable foods and potable water tablets.

- He's serious about barbecue, so don't even hint at the fact that it all tastes the same to you.
- He thinks he's pretty handy and can fix _(fill in the blank)_ , so quietly let him work on it all weekend before discreetly calling the professionals Monday morning.

ABOUT PARENTING

Whether we know it or not, we have in our minds how things are "supposed" to look when raising kids. We also have an idea of how we want to be perceived as parents, both of which go flying out the window within the first few years.

One of my good friends recently volunteered to be the liaison for new families at our school, and she planned a swim party to facilitate the new kids meeting the existing ones. They met at a local swim club and invited all the moms to visit while the kids swam in the pool.

My friend felt like she needed to be in and out of the pool because the kids were young and she wanted to help navigate the waters of new friendships (pun intended). It was close to the end of the swim party when one of her mom friends pulled her aside and mentioned the lower part of her bathing suit was a touch see-through. My friend chalked it up to an Old Navy product that had probably seen its better days and laughed it off.

But upon further inspection, she came to the unfortunate realization that in changing into her tankini earlier in the day, she'd put on the top but never actually switched into her bathing-suit bottom. She had, in fact, been traipsing in and out of the pool all afternoon wearing her nude-colored, very see-through, granny panties. And then, as if it couldn't get worse, when she jumped into her car, so desperate to get out of there, she actually backed right into another car.

I tell you this because even if you haven't worn your granny panties to a swim party, parenting involves a process of revealing parts of ourselves that we didn't even know we had, much less planned on parading about town.

Like marriage, there're some things about parenting that nobody tells you:

- You typically only want parenting advice affirming what you're already doing, so be careful asking for something you may not be ready to receive.
- Always be very careful naming your kids because, one day, when you're labeling a bottle, you'll realize their initials are associated with a marital intimacy product. (Sorry, Kate Yanof.)
- Going from two kids to three kids is amazing, except when it comes to hotel rooms, family vehicles, dinner reservations, and rides at amusement parks.
- Your preschooler reading early will amount to the sum total of nothing by high school, so lay off sharing the developmental milestones if you don't want to get the side-eye.

- Learning to forgive your kids' friends when they hurt your baby is one of the hardest (but necessary) things you'll have to do in parenting.
- Some of the greatest character-developing moments happen during the party your kids weren't invited to.
- Walking out of your kid's dorm room is the hardest yet most rewarding thing you'll find yourself doing someday.

ABOUT TRAVELING

Traveling with small kids. The end.

Okay, not really, but there is a whole "thing" to be aware of when it comes to planning those early family trips. It may seem small in comparison to marriage or parenting, but it's the classic "you don't know what you don't know" … until you do.

Let's take a moment to play a game I like to call "Is it a trip or is it a vacation?" Picture yourself in each of these moments, and then declare "trip" or "vacation" based on your anxiety level and unanticipated perspiration.

- Struggling to pull a wagon full of diapered children wearing copious amounts of sunscreen to the beach? Trip ✔
- Requesting a rollaway, Pack 'n Play, or pullout sofa upon checking in to your resort? Trip ✔

- Attending the family reunion at Aunt Edna's house of trinkets with the only children under ten? Trip ✔
- Booking a VRBO with a fully stocked kitchen and preordering groceries? Trip ✔
- Frantically downloading movies on portable devices in the wee hours before air travel? Trip ✔
- Taking the in-laws? Trip ✔
- Putting one of those enema-shaped storage containers on top of your minivan? Trip ✔
- Engaging in repeated discussions around "expectations" and "prizes" in the weeks leading up to your departure? Trip ✔
- Purchasing matching family Disney shirts? (Not even going to answer this one.)

I must say I do appreciate how *Home Alone* completely lowered the bar on family travel expectations after the parents left Kevin at home TWICE. Not to mention that biblically speaking, Jesus' parents lost Him for more than three days while returning home from Jerusalem.

I'm encouraged that if Joseph and Mary had a parenting fail and lost the Messiah, I can calm the heck down about the Colorado trip where we lost all our groceries (and most of our hanging clothes) out the back of our car in the middle of the Breckenridge roundabout. And then several days later, my husband went all Evel Knievel off a bike jump, which landed him in the ER with broken ribs and a punctured lung (all of which I weirdly got on video in slow motion).

Good memories, that trip, but may it never be called a vacation.

THE TRUTH ABOUT IT ALL

It's easy to miss the bigger picture when you're still figuring out your marriage, raising kids, and balancing the thousands of things that make up everyday family life while planning the next family trip. The truth is, all the seemingly small things end up being the big things, because each of the mishaps, annoyances, and character-building moments are beautifully crafting the very DNA of your family.

You can't see it in the moment, but one day you will wake up to realize the Sonic overreactions serve as the very reminders of just how much your husband loves you, even when you're prone to get slightly crazy over the smallest of things. And even your most embarrassing moments have formed an inseparable bond in your marriage as you both smile when "Sexual Healing" comes on the radio (before instantly changing it because the kids are in the car).

And one sleepless night, you'll be lying in bed (listening to snoring) and remembering the comedy of errors from that ridiculous Colorado trip, suddenly thankful for a husband who is willing to jump off bike ramps all in the name of family fun. You'll be overwhelmed with God's goodness in providing for family trips, even those where your groceries and undergarments end up on display for an entire mountain town to see.

The truth is, all the seemingly small things end up being the big things, because each of the mishaps, annoyances, and character-building moments are beautifully crafting the very DNA of your family.

But there are also the places revealing some of your unsightly parts you intended to keep covered in public. It's right in there in the vulnerability and authenticity where you've found the truest friendships as the layers were peeled back to allow others to walk alongside you in safety and grace.

King David says it so beautifully as he considers the ups and downs of his very complicated life, remarking, "The boundary lines have fallen for me in pleasant places" (Ps. 16:6a).

Yes, they most certainly have.

So when finances are tight, the relatives are difficult, or your kid believes in Santa for way too long, lean into every single bit of it, knowing family is the very dearest thing Jesus has given you. That even the hard things nobody tells you about pale in comparison to how blessed you are with a husband who is trying, a family who is persevering, and a faith that is growing as you walk alongside these people each and every day. And one day in the not-too-distant future, make sure to look back and fully appreciate how pleasantly the boundary lines have truly fallen, and give thanks to the One who authored it all.

CHAPTER 8

The Broom in the Spokes of Your Faith

MESSY TRUTH

What God starts, no person can stop.
What God plans, no obstacle can thwart.
What God wills, no enemy can defeat.

*I*have twin brothers who are five years older than me. While some might write books about how lovely and instrumental their siblings were in their childhood, shaping them into who they are today, giving nostalgic examples of their siblings being their best friends and confidants—that's not this book.

I will preface these next words by saying, I love my brothers wholeheartedly. But these people were real Neanderthals growing up. My mom used to warn them that they would be responsible for paying my counseling bills someday, which had exactly zero impact on their no-holds-barred approach to tormenting me as a child.

I could write pages about their antics because my parents routinely left me in their care. They apparently believed my brothers were responsible. And mature. And trustworthy. Yet over and over again, they proved to be not even a single one of those things. It was never more evident than the time I watched one of them physically eat a piece of paper with my parents' phone number on it so I couldn't call and report my misgivings while they were in charge.

Another time, they left me in a closet all night with a mattress covering me as a safety precaution for a tornado. At first that seems nurturing—my elementary-school self all curled up in a fetal position, waiting out the storm under the protection of a sturdy mattress. But we lived in a town that had not one, but zero, zip, zilch tornadoes in the entire twenty-plus years our family lived in the area.

My brothers were relentless. And to say Baby Jessica falling in the well (if you're too young to remember, Google it) got less 1980s attention than I did the day I got my training bra, well it's true.

May I lament here for a quick second? Why did we insist on this whole training bra charade anyway? What were we training? Was there some moms' code of conduct requiring them to take us to the local Mervyn's to try on the training bras? Were there so many sizing considerations for our little budding selves that it required a department store? Had they declared an "all sales final" policy, making it impractical to do this from the comfort of our homes?

Free with the price of admission at the department store where Dorothy took me was a stranger awkwardly sizing me up while also giving the "sweetie, your body is changing" pep talk through the louvers of the changing room door. In any other context, this is a felony. But there I stood having an out-of-body experience while listening to discussions on breathable fabrics, color choices, and padding considerations. And the cherry on top? Sweet Dorothy insisted I wear this bralette out of the store as if it were a new pair of sporty school shoes.

I arrived home that day in my fatefully paper-thin T-shirt to find my brothers and their equally hideous peers watching MTV from the couch. With the skill of a K-9 in the Miami airport, they sniffed out my parlay into womanhood and topped off my already humiliating day with a healthy dose of puberty mocking and bra-popping.

I share all this mean-brother background to give you some context as to why my bike became my best ally as a child. It was my escape. It was my alone time. It was the wind in my face and the speed beneath my feet. It was also equipped with the cutest little basket for my perfectly placed trinkets. I was my best self each day as I paraded up and down the street freely ringing my bell.

Sadly, my opportunistic brothers were also looking to freely ring my bell. One rather ordinary day, I was pedaling down our street in my most regal manner when my wheels suddenly locked up and my bike came to a screeching halt. Now I need you to picture this: I'm cruising full speed down the street, minding my own business, only to have my wheels completely stop, thereby launching me right off that bike like a long-range missile with a bad Dorothy Hamill haircut.

Turns out my brothers hurled my mother's broom across our driveway, through the street, and directly into the spokes of my bike, using a launch angle even NASA would have applauded.

RIGHT PLACE, WRONG TIME

My bicycle debacle was a wrong place, wrong time kind of catastrophe. I've suffered similar brooms to the spokes of my faith. Situations that felt like the wrong place at the wrong time that brought me to an equally jarring stop. At times it's been small things like annoyances, obstacles, and setbacks that have discouraged me from pursuing the God-ordained opportunities in front of me. Other times it's been battling an imposter syndrome of feeling underqualified and overlooked in comparison with those who *really have* God's favor.

I'm reminded of the story of Joseph. His brothers sold him into slavery and lied to their father about his death because they were jealous he was their father's favorite. (Those are some mean brothers who put even mine to shame.) Yet in the midst of slavery, Joseph found favor with the captain of Pharaoh's guard and went from slave status to landing a power position in Potiphar's house. Unfortunately, he also found favor with Potiphar's wife, who tried unsuccessfully to seduce him. That landed him in jail; however, Pharaoh began having bad dreams, and Joseph had the God-given ability to interpret them. Eventually, Joseph was released from prison and promoted to second-in-command under Pharaoh.

Joseph had every right to give up, throw up his hands in discouragement, and question all that God was allowing in his life. But instead of questioning God, he continued to pray, and trust, and put one foot in front of the other, until one day famine swept their land, and Pharaoh had extra rations (thanks to Joseph). Joseph's brothers came to Egypt for grain but left with forgiveness and, in a full-circle moment, Joseph said these life-changing words: "you intended to harm me, but God intended it for good" (Gen. 50:20a).

That's the thing about God's favor. It doesn't typically look very favorable in the moment. Mark Batterson describes it this way: "God is in the business of strategically positioning us in the right place at the right time. But here's the catch: The right place often seems like the *wrong* place, and the right time often seems like the *wrong* time."[1]

Somewhere along the way, I mistakenly grabbed on to the idea that having God on my side and allowing Him to work through my life meant things would look a certain way. An easy way. I thought people would support me, circumstances would work out easily, and obstacles would elude me. After all, I'm trying to do the God things (most of the time).

But a quick glance in the Old Testament reminds us that God's favor almost always looks different from my preferred definition of favor. I enjoy favor when it comes in the form of job opportunities, financial gain, increased significance, and easy roads to walk. And believing this to be the case, when my circumstances don't prove particularly favorable, I'm prone to think God turned a blind eye or somehow I've misinterpreted God's will.

That's the thing about God's favor. It doesn't typically look very favorable in the moment.

But God's favor oftentimes includes long years of infertility (Abraham), leading groups of people who don't respect you (Moses), being martyred by a culture that rejects your faith (all but one disciple), or even watching those who are closest to you turn against you (Joseph).

Honestly, God's favor oftentimes feels anything but favorable in the moment. His protection feels like punishment, and His greatest plans will likely come at the expense of our comfort, our personal advancement, and our best laid out timelines. Great news, right? (Said with complete sarcasm.)

Joseph's life models the long game of following God. It's up, it's down, it's sometimes hard, and it's often inexplicable. But in the end, when it's all said and done, Joseph saw his life through God's lens and realized that without mean brothers there was no slavery, and without slavery there was no Potiphar, and without Potiphar there was no prison, and without prison there was no Pharaoh, and without Pharaoh there was no grain and reconciliation.

Or said differently, what God starts, no person can stop. What God begins, no delay can circumvent. What God plans, no obstacle can thwart. What God wills, no enemy can defeat.

KNOCKED DOWN, NOT OUT

Just this week, I woke up to something that was super discouraging. Literally, not one other person in the entire world would have noticed it, but it stuck out like a sore thumb to me. It was buried in an email thousands of people received, but it sparked reminders of some hard things in my past that continue to feel like a real threat to my future. It's simply a roadblock. But there are some days when our roadblocks feel more like highway closures than simple detours.

It's actually slightly comical.

From the moment I woke up and looked at my phone (perhaps the problem), I was stewing. When I say this situation stuck out to me like a sore thumb, I mean it quite literally. I had a bunch of stitches in my thumb because, apparently, distractedly dicing onions is dangerous. And it's near impossible to scroll through my phone, let alone text with one thumb—so that's a journey in and of itself. But let's not activate the prayer chain or send out the Meal Train just yet.

As I went about my morning routine and then drove to my favorite place to write, I couldn't let it go. I fumed thinking about this unjust situation (the email, not my thumb). I pondered what kind of response I might give to avenge myself and mentally ironed out my "position" for a big confrontation that would probably never come about.

I noticed unusually heavy traffic at one particular intersection, and this too annoyed me. As I got closer to the intersection, I saw the road was completely blocked off for construction. That was just God being funny, meeting my roadblock with a roadblock.

Turning the corner (literally and figuratively), I asked the Lord to give me a word of assurance that He was with me and saw this hard situation facing me. It felt big. It felt ominous. It felt like God had called me to do something with virtually no opportunity for success because the roadblocks were significant and the obstacles seemed insurmountable.

But as I got situated and checked my email before hunkering down to write this chapter, I ran across a different email I had sent to myself the day before. It contained lyrics from a Christian song playing in the car on our way to church. The email was blank other than these words: "When all I see is the battle, You see my victory."[2]

I wished I could go back and reverse the order in which I read my emails that morning. I needed to start my day off remembering the battle is already won, even if it didn't feel victorious in the moment. In Revelation we're told, "What he opens no one can shut, and what he shuts no one can open" (Rev. 3:7b).

We may be knocked down, but we aren't knocked out. I feel this so deeply because the opportunity to write this very book has come on the heels of the biggest disappointment and door-closing situation I've ever faced, professionally or personally.

Yet I'm reminded of how quickly I'm willing to assign power to things that are powerless over my life. I assume the final say is with those whom God no longer allows a voice in my life. I fear a road closing when it's simply God's rerouting.

Mark Batterson says it this way: "I've come to think of closed doors as divine detours. And while our failed plans can be incredibly discouraging and disorienting, God often uses the things that seem to be taking us off our course to keep us on *His* course."[3]

Someday I'll be face to face with Jesus, watching my life on heaven's big screen with instant replay. And when we get to the parts that have felt like brooms in the spokes of my faith, I believe the full story will be revealed, and I too will say, "What was intended for harm, God used for good."

CHAPTER 9

Going the Distance

MESSY TRUTH

Jesus was too busy building a ministry
to build a platform, which is a reminder
that God's most important work in our
lives doesn't require an audience.

nyone who tells you there's no purgatory hasn't taught a teenage boy to drive.

What these boys lack in common sense, they make up for in high-octane, testosterone-induced swagger. That's neither a compliment nor a recipe for successful driving; it's just the reality.

They are infantile.
They are dangerous.
They should be a protected class.

Think about it: our country is rightfully set up in such a way that we don't allow fifteen-year-old boys to do virtually anything of significance.

Why?

Because they are squirrely, and ridiculous, and if we're being honest … a little bit weird.

I can think of at least ten things in this country that we *do not* allow fifteen-year-olds to do because we are grown adults, and smart, and make the rules. But here are just a few examples.

1. **Vote.** Nope, you don't get to be part of naming the most powerful leader in the free world for many reasons, not the least of which is you leave your athletic cup on our kitchen table.
2. **Join the military.** We'll pass on allowing the freedoms promised by Washington, Jefferson, and Hamilton to be upheld by those who belch the alphabet in the shower.

3. **Donate blood.** Absolutely not, because we've seen your dances go viral on TikTok, and if fifteen is contagious, we can't handle another pandemic.

4. **Buy a lottery ticket.** That's a hard pass because there are only so many subwoofers, lift kits, and LED undercarriage lights our infrastructure can handle when teen boys have extra cash.

5. **Become an organ donor.** Thank you for the extremely kind gesture, but with almost 100% certainty we will pass on your innards based on the explanations above.

So if none of these things are considered developmentally appropriate for the teen boy, who is the genius that thought it was a good idea to let him drive?

Seriously, you can't even get a Costco card or operate a deli slicer at the grocery store until you're eighteen—because buying in bulk or losing a pinky is somehow riskier than my son cueing up "Smells Like Teen Spirit" while operating a moving vehicle.

You can't even act as a notary public in this country at sixteen, yet nobody seems to grapple with throwing our teenage boys behind four thousand pounds of steel each day.

Hold up there, Johnny. No way you're witnessing me sign a deed of trust, but let's take my $30K vehicle out for a spin with no way for me to brake, steer, or otherwise change your course or direction.

Maybe I'm the weird one, but I just find it ironic that we're busy over here debating whether alopecia is slap-worthy (just a little

Will Smith humor), while permits are freely being handed out to pubescent boys.

(I say "freely handed out," but anyone who has braved the Department of Public Safety knows that Peter walking on water ain't got nothing on the miracle of gathering all the necessary paperwork to get your kid a permit on the first try. Amirite?)

I assume it goes without saying that I'm currently in the throes of teaching my own fifteen-year-old son, Brett, to drive. I need breathing exercises. Or maybe a therapy dog. And there's not enough Xanax in the world to calm my shot nerves as he repeatedly goes 60 mph through our neighborhood and 20 mph on the highway.

Weaving. Swerving. Hitting curbs. Following too close. And just when I'm jolted out of my scared stupor to yell "you have to yield there!"— I'm met with a surly "your mama has to yield there."

Awesome.

THE RADIUS OF JESUS

At times when I'm teaching Brett to drive, I can't help but think of Jesus. Mostly because I'm one lane change away from meeting Him at any given moment. But still. I think about the amount of time Jesus spent patiently teaching His disciples. He meticulously and persistently grounded them in the same lessons over and over about who He was, why He came, the significance of following Him, and what it looked like to love others well.

I chuckle thinking about how He explained the upside-down kingdom of God to them, and that the first will be last and the last will be first. How loving God means living with humility, and that pride will surely lead to our demise. And then a breath later He overheard the disciples arguing about which of them would be the greatest in heaven. I've got to believe He wanted to bang His omniscient head against the wall sometimes.

He was a teacher at heart. And even though He never experienced teaching teen boys how to drive, He spent His earthly life teaching twelve young men how to live well. It seems in doing so He was less interested in the distance the disciples might go and more in how they walked the miles they were given. It makes sense considering the radius of Jesus' ministry was only one hundred or so miles—less than most of us drive in a given week.

But it's what He did in those one hundred miles that changed the world forever.

Jesus walked thousands of miles within that one-hundred-mile radius, teaching humility, and kindness, and how to love God by loving those He puts in our paths. It was miles of healing the brokenhearted while rebuking the hard-hearted. It was confronting and correcting the religious elite while showing compassion for the marginalized. There were sermons, miracles, and one particularly fiery exchange in the temple that served as a warning for those who use the church for the wrong reasons.

Jesus wanted His disciples to go the distance well, however long or short that might end up being. And as I teach my son to drive and worry about his gaping incompetence, I find myself praying that he too might do life well.

I think of things like influence. It can be confusing—in a world that measures influence by the size of your following—to remember that Jesus only had twelve close followers. He was too busy building a ministry to build a platform, which is a reminder that God's most important work in our lives doesn't require a big audience.

Or even the notion that you have to go far to make a difference in this world. If Jesus' ministry was focused on the one hundred miles closest to where He resided, then our biggest impact is likely in our neighborhoods, workplaces, and at home as we love our spouses unconditionally and train our children biblically.

And then there's the hyperfocus on safety. I remember when my own parents taught me to drive, they threw out the adage that "most wrecks happen within a few miles of your house." In my most snarky teenage voice, I suggested that if this were in fact true, we should consider moving. (Apparently teenage girls are not that much better than teenage boys.)

But most accidents do happen close to home because those are the roads we travel the most. Jesus' disciples learned pretty quickly that walking the road with Jesus was anything but safe, yet it was significant. I'm guessing that became especially clear as they watched Him walk the road to Calvary.

Francis Chan talks about safety this way:

> We are consumed by safety. Obsessed with it, actually. Now I'm not saying it is wrong to pray for God's protection, but I am questioning how we've made safety our highest priority. We've

elevated safety to the neglect of whatever God's best is, whatever would bring God the most glory, or whatever would accomplish His purposes in our lives and in the world.[1]

Yes, I'll pray for my son's safety every day, because I'm all too aware of how much he needs it. But if living safely comes at the price of Brett knowing Jesus better, that's a price I hope he's never willing to pay.

WHAT ARE YOU DOING FOR THE LORD?

And so in teaching my son to drive well, I'm left hoping he also learns how to live well. Just as Jesus changed the world by living big in a small radius, I pray that Brett will leave his God-given mark (preferably not tire tracks) no matter where the road takes him. But to do so means giving everything he's got to the Lord and trusting Him to use it in ways he could never do on his own.

This reminds me of a man named David Green, who once told me how all his life his parents had asked him this one pivotal question: What are you doing for the Lord?

He came from a modest family with a preacher dad and lots of siblings. They had very little financially, but his parents drilled into deep territory spiritually. As David moved out of the house and began to see success in his career, his parents would always congratulate him but then immediately ask what he was doing for the Lord.

If Jesus' ministry was focused on the one hundred miles closest to where He resided, then our biggest impact is likely in our neighborhoods, workplaces, and at home as we love our spouses unconditionally and train our children biblically.

After many years of prayer and hard work, David Green went from managing retail stores, to owning stores, to becoming the largest privately owned art-and-crafters retailer in the world. Today Hobby Lobby grosses over eight billion dollars a year and gives roughly 50 percent of their earnings to charity.[2] All that while also paying their employees well above minimum wage, filling their stores with Christian music, and closing every Sunday so their employees can have a day of rest.

I guess his life answers the question of what he's doing for the Lord.

I think about David Green's parents, who had no way of knowing their small-town son, who struggled in school, didn't attend college, and loved working at a five-and-dime, would someday be called a "biblical billionaire" by *Forbes*.[3]

But God did.

Just like …

- Moses's mom didn't know the baby she left in the river would one day lead an entire people out of slavery.
- Abraham's mom didn't know one day her son would travel to a foreign land and become the father of many nations.
- Joseph's mom didn't know that sibling rivalry would one day end in reconciliation and forgiveness.
- Mary's mom didn't know that one day her daughter would give birth to the Messiah.

And I don't know what our squirrely fifteen-year-old son, who makes "your mama" jokes while driving recklessly around town, will be called to do in his life. But God does.

As we teach the next generation to drive or tie their shoes or pack for college, may we always remember the bigger goal of teaching them how to live well. Reminding them that God is less interested in the distance they will go than in how well they walk (or drive) the miles they are given.

And with each success they see, may we be faithful to follow up with one critically important question: What are you doing for the Lord?

CHAPTER 10

Waiting for Our Future

MESSY TRUTH

If today is the only day we're promised, let's
refuse to spend another day waiting for the right
time, permission, or some arbitrary must-have
before doing the God things of significance.

*Y*ou may have already figured this out, but I was a lawyer at one time.

No seriously, it was a short little stint and not illustrious by anyone's account, but nevertheless it happened.

Let's not go all Bob Goff about this, thinking I was conducting witch trials in Uganda and using my legal prowess to chip away at the world's social injustices. Nope, I worked in a downtown Dallas law firm and represented big companies in my Ann Taylor suits with shoulder pads and nude hose. Jealous, right?

Now there are a few things I need to discuss with those of you who have never darkened a law school door. First of all, law students say really dumb things like "That's a tort" when someone accidentally bumps into your grocery cart.

Or, "Possession is nine-tenths of the law" as they snatch your wallet off the kitchen table.

Or, "I plead the Fifth" when asked what they did on a date the night before.

It's marginally insufferable.

But then you give a barely graduated law student a big fat office with a view, and they start saying even dumber things that I'm not going to detail here. Sadly, you will inevitably find it sprinkled throughout my writing because I can't even help myself. (I'll bold the unnecessary legal references so we can make a **#DumbThingsLawyersSay** hashtag someday.)

I was one of the best mediocre lawyers of my day.

By far my greatest legal victory was meeting my husband, Mike—a truly amazing attorney—in law school. My second finest achievement came in the many friendships formed at that same downtown Dallas law firm. That's where I met my dear friend Elaine, who was and is the very best of what the legal world has to offer.

We met as young lawyers, officed next door to each other, and had way too much fun, as many partners in our firm would later **attest** to.

Let me give you a **primer** on practicing law as a defense lawyer: You are required to meet certain **billable hour** requirements, meaning every minute of your workday matters and needs to be accounted for. So when you're not working, you're not billing hours, you're not making money for the firm, you're not doing your job, and, well, that's a problem.

But refusing to be held back by that minutiae, Elaine and I set out to be the best of the best when it came to having fun. It started with little squirrely things like sending email **inquiries** to the managing partner asking for his whereabouts on days when his office light was off. And then there was the afternoon we spent making approved CPR lists to **ensure** there were no mouth-to-mouth mishaps should we have a health crisis during office hours. Ain't nobody who wants to "come to" only to find themselves locking lips with Al from accounting.

One time we were assigned to a fairly serious project out of state that required sifting through endless boxes of documents until one lost the will to live. Picture a large, very quiet room full of lawyers looking at seemingly important information. Elaine and I took it upon ourselves to very courteously (yet forcefully) cough each time an attorney picked up a new box of documents in the front of the room just in case an unexpected flatulent slipped out. We called it a courtesy cough, obviously, and nobody laughed like we did.

Actually, nobody laughed at all.

Case in point of our fabulous antics came the time that we ordered Victoria's Secret catalogs to be delivered to all the male partners at their firm address. Oh, and then a few weeks later we decided we wanted to make some money. No, literally we set out to prove that currency couldn't be that hard to print, so we took the afternoon (and the firm's color copiers) for a **discovery** exercise of sorts. Ironically, it is in fact "that hard" to print currency—not to mention a federal crime. Moving on.

They called us the dynamic duo. We traveled all over the country together for work, and then it became couples' vacations, and holidays, and our weddings, and having our babies. We were fun, we were somewhat irreverent, and we were undaunted by the stuffy norms of our law firm back in the day.

Turns out Elaine became a remarkable lawyer once I left the firm to stay home with my babies. Not only did she make partner but she helped many clients through their hardest legal issues. She was kind and funny and genuine and a welcomed breath of fresh air in an oftentimes incredibly stressful environment. She was also beautiful, inside and out, with a killer sense of fashion and the most incredible wit of any person I've ever known.

As much as I could go on for days and days telling stories about my sweet friend Elaine, it's her background that tells the real story. As a daughter of immigrants, Elaine knew her parents risked everything by leaving their extended family, their home, and their security to load their four kids on a boat from Vietnam to the United States. Although they were financially depleted when they set foot in America, they were brimming with hope in the American dream and the endless opportunities available for their children and their future.

Shortly after they arrived in the United States, a small Baptist church in Palestine, Texas, adopted their family. This precious church moved Elaine's family to a little house in a little town, giving them a big chance for new beginnings. And spoiler alert: Fast-forward forty-plus years and these same four kids have grown up to be amazing adults who went to amazing colleges (including Harvard) and became four unbelievable success stories, including three lawyers and one highly skilled businessman.

PROMISING FUTURE OR CHERISHED PRESENT

Elaine's family refers to her as their glue—the one who keeps everyone together. I recently realized she was the glue not just for her immediate family but, as I looked around a room packed with people, for so many others she'd touched. Person after person had traveled from all over the country to attend Elaine's funeral celebrating a beautiful life cut way too short. Way, way too short.

It was surreal listening to her two amazing teenage children speak so eloquently having just lost their precious mom. I watched her husband choke out every word of his eulogy determined to honor the woman whom he loved so extravagantly. And then there was picture after picture in the slideshow featuring my beautiful friend traveling, parenting, working, **advocating**, and connecting so many people, because that's just who she was. Every picture was a reminder of how fully and fiercely she loved her people.

Now if I might interrupt this moving moment to mention one **sidebar** item of interest from attending this funeral with my precious husband. As I watched the slideshow, it hit me like a ton of bricks the sheer number of pictures they had of Elaine with her family. It also reminded me that I take *all* the pics of our family on vacations (as do you), and I'm in none of them.

None.

It's as if I haven't gone on a vacation with my family in years, and I rarely make time to even drop in at their birthday celebrations. My daughter Kate, even joking about this **truism**, occasionally calls me over during the holidays or vacation for a "slideshow" pic (as she calls it) for my funeral someday. My husband apparently was equally struck by the number of pictures of Elaine on display, because right there in the service he leaned over to the guy to my left and asked if he would take a quick shot of the two of us. Bless it.

Near the end of Elaine's service, an older woman approached the mic to speak. She was from the First Baptist Church of Palestine, Texas—the church that sponsored Elaine's family when they arrived in the United States more than forty years ago. This woman shared stories of meeting Elaine and her family in that small East Texas town, helping them settle into their little home, and meeting their needs despite significant language barriers. She said the church fell in love with beautiful Elaine, her tiny smile, her big personality, and her three doting brothers and loving parents.

I found myself tearing up as I heard stories of this little church loading up Elaine and her brothers each Sunday morning on the church bus, taking them to Sunday school and services, then delivering them back home. Little Elaine had only one church dress to her name, but she wore it proudly each week as she jumped onto that bus with her brothers and headed to the neighborhood church that claimed them as their own.

I continue to be moved by the kind of faith that doesn't stop at showing up once to provide a little relief for a family in need but that, time and time again, expresses love with the simplicity of an old church bus and a community of believers determined to love their neighbors.

It's uncomplicated. It's unremarkable. It's unusual.

Looking back on Elaine's gift of "glue" for so many, I'm reminded of the intentionality she showed in her friendships. Remarkably, Elaine was the best connector of people I have ever known, yet she had not one social media account. I guess she understood what I so often do not: no amount of scrolling and liking can replicate the gift of simply showing up.

Her showing up was nothing unheard of or crazy. It was just simple texts making sure we scheduled lunch or a quick call to see if my daughter was happy in college. It was thoughtful gifts like the tie she bought my husband when he **made partner** or the diapers she dropped off when we started fostering.

It's a challenge to do less so we can be more to those whom God has entrusted to us.

And then there's the cross necklace she gave me for my birthday and the personalized stationery delivered just weeks before her death—these are my tangible reminders of the importance of loving people unconditionally and intentionally as long as I have the breath to do so. Because even though Elaine and I didn't vote the same, parent the same, look the same, or even begin life in the same country, commonality wasn't a condition she placed on loving those around her well.

Elaine's life has challenged me to do more. Or maybe it's a challenge to *do less* so we can *be more* to those whom God has entrusted to us. Elaine didn't inherently have more time than the rest of us— turns out she actually had less time than any of us could have ever imagined. But she made the most of her time as if somehow grasping Solomon's warning that life's a vapor, **thereby** leaving no time to waste on the insignificant.

Elaine's husband wrote the most beautiful obituary I've ever read. In it he noted that several years before her death, she made the hard decision to "walk away from her 'promising future' as a lawyer to live her 'cherished present' as a mother."

What a difficult decision it must have been for Elaine to leave her **law practice**. But then again, hard decisions were woven into her very fabric by parents who braved an ocean by boat to pursue a better life for their family.

I'm reminded of the many places where we're so prone to wait on a "promising future" instead of living in our "cherished present." As we wait for God to give us a spouse, the child we've always wanted, close friendships, better health, dream jobs, the right neighborhood, a second home, increased significance, a better marriage, or maybe a bestselling book.

If today is the only day we're promised, let's refuse to spend another day waiting for the right time or for permission or for some arbitrary must-have with no eternal significance. Let's follow Elaine's lead, and

send the text
plan the trip
buy the gift
write the letter
scroll less
apologize more
let it go
live it up
refuse to worry
find the fun
live big
cherish the small

And by all means, may we treasure our days on this side of heaven and use them to love others like there's no tomorrow. Because someday there won't be.

CHAPTER 11

A Groovy Kind of Love

MESSY TRUTH

I wonder how different our love would look if we fully understood the Jesus who leaves the ninety-nine for the one, and we are the one.

*M*y dad is a character.

People say I get my sense of humor from him. It's not just the words he speaks or the jokes he makes, but even the things he does are funny. My mom tells a story of when my brothers were toddlers and unbelievably loud and boisterous. It was double trouble because, with identical twins, everything is magnified by two. Particularly problematic was riding in the car and keeping them quiet and stationary.

This was back before the days of car seats with five-point harnesses and anchors built into the structure of our cars. It was the '70s, and people were just groovy enough to let their kids roam all willy-nilly in the car for a quick trip to the grocery store or even a longer trip to Grandma's. Sure, the more rule-following kids stayed buckled in their seats and observed basic safety protocols. But the wilder types, like my brothers, were often found cruising around the car haphazardly, causing my mom to go to extraordinary lengths to keep them alive while simply trying to get to Wednesday night church.

I'm guessing you can probably relate to this even today. While some adults might brace when traffic stops for fear of another car hitting them or their seat belts locking—not those of us from the '70s. We still brace for the impact of Mom's arm flying across the front seat and hitting us square in the chest in an antiquated, yet equally violent, version of an airbag deployment.

Because my brothers were loud and wild toddlers (and teenagers), my dad decided he had to do something to make family car rides more pleasant. At the time, he worked in the car business, and as a perk he had opportunities to purchase all makes and models at a reduced price. So he went on a mission to find the perfect car to meet the needs of our growing family while also meeting his need for a little bit of peace and quiet on the open roads.

As luck would have it, one day he came across a new ride promising to solve all our car-traveling dilemmas. He instantly knew it was a no-brainer for our family, so he opted out of the phone call discussions and test drive protocols that typically included my mom with such a large purchase. He was so convinced she was going to love it as much as he did, he paid for the car sight unseen (by my mom) and immediately called her to announce his big surprise for that evening.

After work, he pulled up in front of their modest home and honked a few times to get my mom's attention. His excitement was palpable as he sat waiting for her to come outside and lay eyes on his genius purchase. And so out of their little house my mom came, with a little boy balanced on each hip, ready for a big reveal promising to change her driving experience forever.

It was as if time stood still as my mom took a long, emotionless look at her new car. My dad waited in anticipation for her response, until finally their eyes locked. And in that moment, there were no words necessary to convey my mom's unmistakable response: under no circumstances would she be driving this *hearse*.

In an instant he knew he had made a *grave* mistake. But even so, the rationale for buying his family a funeral home hearse still sort of made sense in his head. This particular hearse had a retractable window behind the front seats, allowing one to close it at any point in time and instantly gain silence and privacy all with the touch of a button.

What seemed genius to my father was appalling to my mother, and with nary a kick of the tires or a family ride around the block, my father returned the car.

WHAT'S LOVE GOT TO DO WITH IT?

Although my dad's love has not always been typical, it's always been tangible.

He's never been one to give sentimental speeches or enjoy long bear hug greetings. He doesn't gush with emotion or even close each conversation with a heartfelt "I love you." But he's shown me genuine love is far more than an emotion; it's an action. And he's been acting on his love toward others for as long as I can possibly remember.

I've watched him push the wheelchair of a widow's daughter to their car each and every Sunday after church. I've seen him spend evenings and weekends volunteering his handyman skills to replace garbage disposals and repair toilets. He's served ice cream at church functions, taught countless Sunday school lessons, and given freely of his finances even when it has cost him significantly. Time and time again, I've watched him serve others quietly with no expectation or applause, because that's just the way he's wired when it comes to loving those he calls his own.

I think this is how Jesus wants us to show our love. He tells us to love Him by loving those around us. He doesn't give us a list of the right words or approved agendas; He just asks us to love our neighbors freely and frequently without counting the cost.

Jesus didn't give long speeches explaining how we're to love; He just lived it. As He walked each day, He loved those He encountered in ways that were less sentimental and more practical. He loved them through His actions far more than words alone ever could have accomplished.

He didn't reason with His friends when their brother died; He just wept. He didn't scorn the woman at the well in her shame; He just offered living water. He didn't judge the paralytic for not getting to the pool; He just healed him. He didn't complain about the wasted perfume; He just cherished it.

I think maybe the reason Jesus taught us to love practically instead of simply emotionally is because He knew there would be times when we lacked the right words. This practical side of love doesn't even get identified with love sometimes. It's just doing things so regularly and willingly that others don't even think to call it love—it's just you. It's an "as you go" kind of love that comes with no explanation or expectation.

No, I don't have long letters with fancy words proving my dad's love. I don't have expensive gifts from him memorializing my biggest milestones. But I do have a storehouse of memories with a dad who rode dirt bikes with us, repaired high school cars for us, walked our newborn babies in front of us, and a lifetime of knowing he unconditionally supported us.

My dad's love has been an invaluable gift of being present, helpful, and available. That's the love Jesus desires for all of us: not expensive or eloquent, but always extravagant.

FIRE AND RAIN

When I was little, my parents attended a tiny Baptist church in the Texas Panhandle. The town was rather stagnant and, sadly, so was the church. The programs were small. The visitors were few. And the inspiration was lacking. This church was in desperate need of CPR, and the members of the church were all too aware of it.

My parents gathered with a group of people from their church and began praying for the Lord to set their church on fire. They needed revival, and nothing short of God's hand was going to bring it. And a few days before Christmas, my parents received a call that their little Baptist church was, actually, on fire.

Half wondering if this was God's literal answer to a figurative prayer against complacency, they ran up to the church as crews were working to put out the fire. Nobody was in the building that night, so thankfully the only damage was to the church property. They later found out the fire started with a Christmas candle on the choir banister, which an unattended child had lit earlier that evening. (I'm thinking that had the work of a preacher's kid written all over it.)

My mom was active in the church's music program, including playing the handbells in the handbell choir. Baptists love handbells like Methodists love an early Sunday lunch, so once the fire was out, my mom panicked remembering the handbells were still in a building filled with water that would ruin them.

The music minister was out of town, so my mom asked a firefighter if he would assist my dad in going into the building to retrieve the handbells. Now in what world does a firefighter agree to let some random person enter a recently burning building on a freezing night in December to retrieve handbells? I don't know. But he agreed to accompany my dad in the pitch black through a basement filled with water because, after all, hadn't they already lost enough?

My dad tells this part of the story like a good fishing story. What was once a few inches of water on the church basement floor, has over the years turned into him swimming in the Arctic all in the name of saving the bells. But either way, the mission was accomplished and my mom was thrilled to secure the bells, even at the cost of my wet and freezing father.

But the story doesn't end there. After a few minutes my mother realized that one single bell was still missing. Everyone knows: a handbell choir you have not if a bell is missing. And so my dad went back into the once burning building, trudging through water, and retrieved the single missing bell. A few days later, the local paper published an article all about how "Dorothy Wilkinson Saved the Bells" with absolutely no mention of my dad. He's still talking about that one.

But going back to save just one isn't a story unique to my earthly father; it's also the story of our heavenly Father.

What I mean is that, in a funny kind of way, my dad going in after the one rogue handbell reminds me of the kind of love Jesus showed on the cross. We tend to think of His sacrifice as a community project that happened to include us but wasn't an act of love uniquely on our behalf.

I wonder how different our love would look if we really understood our oneness in Jesus. If we lived and loved others from an overflow of gratitude for the One who would leave the ninety-nine to save just one. And we are the one.

Your neighbor is also the one. And your boss is the one. And your mother-in-law is the one. And the guy who lets his dog do his business in your front yard without cleaning up—he too is the one.

How would a culture selling a love that's conditional, temporary, and earned respond to such a different version of love? How

I wonder how different our love would look if we really understood our oneness in Jesus. If we lived and loved others from an overflow of gratitude for the One who would leave the ninety-nine to save just one. And we are the one.

might we see people differently, love people differently, serve people differently in this very moment if we basked in this kind of love?

NIGHT COMETH

The church Mike and I have attended for many years has a bell-tower clock with the words "Night Cometh" inscribed across it. It's a visual cue that one day our lights will dim this side of heaven and we will be faced with the realities of eternity. Our church sits in a part of town with amazing restaurants and some of the best shopping in the country—reminding me not to get complacent in earthly comforts, but to do today what I'm not guaranteed the chance to do tomorrow.

Understandably, there's not a one of us who cares to think about the day when it's all said and done and we're on our final ride in my dad's problem-solving vehicle of choice. But "Night Cometh" is a challenge to live each day with fewer words and more actions. The kind of love my dad has lived for eighty-plus years in a hearse buying, handbell saving, no cost counted, no recognition seeking kind of way.

That's the kind of love I want to live. Jesus' version of love.

CHAPTER 12

ThighMasters and God's Voice

MESSY TRUTH

It's in God's very nature to speak to us, but as our world gets busier, and noisier, and harder, it simply takes a little more intentionality to hear Him.

*I*t was just a few weeks before Christmas, and to say we were anxious would be a massive understatement. There's something about Christmastime and all the decorations and celebrations that makes it that much harder when you're facing potentially devastating news. Our family was trying to pretend everything was normal, but an ominous cloud was making it especially difficult to go through the motions of the holidays.

In the coming days we were to find out the permanent resolution of our first foster care placement. It was a countdown to see whether JB would remain in our home or if he would be removed. The big hearing had been rescheduled several times for various reasons, and the uncertainty of his future had become more and more excruciating. He had been in our home for more than eighteen months, and to say he had become part of our family, well, there are no words. With this precious little boy's future in the balance, we had an army of people praying for the judge, as she was about to make this very permanent decision for JB's life.

During the months while we were doing foster care, our best friends were attending a small church across town. They had asked this little community of believers to pray over our family each week, and they had linked arms and done just that for many months.

The night before the final hearing date, the anxiety was high (and honestly, the dread was off the charts too). Our friends called to ask if their pastor, Pierre Jones, could come to our home and pray with us before the judge ruled the next day. Although we had never met this pastor or attended his church before, we agreed to have him come pray with us after Kate's Christmas choir concert.

When we arrived home late that evening, Pastor Pierre was waiting in his car. Even knowing we had arrived home, he allowed a significant amount of time to pass before he came inside to join us. We exchanged pleasantries and then got ready to pray. I'll never forget standing there in a circle with our dear friends, their kids, our family, and Pastor Pierre—feeling physically sick knowing that, in all likelihood, this precious baby I was cradling would be leaving us the next day. The stark contrast between the joyous Christmas decorations in our house and the heaviness in our hearts will stay with me forever.

But as we were about to begin praying, Pastor Pierre stopped us and very thoughtfully said God had spoken a word to him that he needed to share. As he was praying outside our house that night, the Lord told him this baby was created to be ours. While acknowledging his words were quite bold, he went on to say the Lord told him we did not need to pray for the result of the hearing tomorrow or spend the night anxiously awaiting what might happen with this little boy's future. Instead, we were to simply praise God for what was already done: JB was going to be our son.

Now to be honest, I've never had someone speak so prophetically to me in God's name, and I would be lying to say it didn't cross my mind that Pastor Pierre might have just committed the biggest doctrinal snafu of a lifetime. After all, the rubber would meet the road the next day when the judge ruled, and that would be an interesting faith discussion to have with our kids if the pastor was wrong. But there was a confidence and authority in his word from the Lord that left us no option but to follow his lead and give thanks for what the Lord had already done for JB and our family.

After we parted ways that evening and as I rocked JB a few extra minutes before putting him in his crib, I thanked the Lord for the kind of man who would show up and pray for people he's never met. I thanked Him for a pastor who had a million other things he could be doing during the Christmas holidays, but was willing to drive across a big city because the Lord called him to do it. And I thanked the Lord for someone who had learned to listen for God's voice and then confidently relay a message that would likely change our lives forever.

LACKING COMPASSION BUT GAINING MUSCLE MEMORY

I was a psychology major in college. I wasn't sure what I wanted to be when I grew up, but it was definitely not a psychologist or psychiatrist because people's problems got on my nerves. It seems insensitive now that I'm actually typing it, but I pictured my future filled with patients lying on my couch, looking at inkblot images, trying to find answers to their deepest childhood problems. Constantly asking "How does that make you feel" made *me* feel like I had better pursue a different career path. (And let's be honest, God gave me plenty of giftings, but He may have skimped just a bit in the compassion category.)

Majoring in psychology when you don't care to deal with other people's problems is a tenuous career path at best. So, by default, I decided I "might as well" go to law school. (For what it's worth, the apple doesn't fall far from the academic tree, as my daughter is currently majoring in journalism and wants little to do with the media. She too, by default, is thinking she "might as well" go to law school.)

My parents were a bit nervous about my lack of psychological aspirations since they were paying a fortune for college and all that. So one summer when I was home, they set me up with a job working for a doctor friend of theirs. I appreciate their moxie, thinking I might change my major and become a physician someday, but what they failed to appreciate is that a lack of compassion is the Achilles' heel of a medical professional.

Nonetheless, I looked real cute showing up to my first day of work in my best professional attire (which was too short, too tight, and altogether unprofessional by any other working person's standards). It hit me as I walked up a few minutes late: I didn't take time to ask what kind of doctor I would be working for. I was hoping for the kind of doctor that pays a lot and works a little.

Soon enough, though, I learned he was a general practitioner, treating everything from routine coughs and colds to more personal matters like annual exams. Yes, women's annual exams. It might be appropriate to stop here for a moment of silence on how this was about to play out.

My first few weeks I worked the front desk answering phone calls, checking in patients, and photocopying insurance cards. I quickly decided that sick people were downers, so I got proficient at checking them in, updating their paperwork, and seating them with all their infirmities and such as far across the room from me as possible.

One particular day, a patient came in with stomach issues, and just as he was signing in to see the doctor, he lost his lunch. I mean lost it all over my little desk, my Big Gulp, and even my unprofessional-professional attire. I'll limit the details since you don't want them, and I don't know them, because I literally jumped up from my desk and ran outside to sit on the back steps of the office.

(Compassionate, I know.)

I'm not sure how much time passed before the doctor came out and sat by me on the steps. He was way too kind for the likes of someone like me. He patiently explained how people who go to the doctor are oftentimes, well, sick, and it was our job to help them feel better. I even vaguely remember some tired discussion about me trying to be more gracious. But what started out as a good old-fashioned mentoring moment quickly took a dark turn when he announced "perhaps it was time I got more of a 'bird's-eye' view of his work."

Sadly, the bird's eye landed on some poor lady's annual exam later that same afternoon. Not coincidentally, it also became the day I stopped associating stirrups with an '80s fashion trend. And perhaps it wasn't ideal that I visibly cringed with each reference to lumps, paps, ovaries, and speculums. But it was in those few moments I gained a brand-new appreciation for how people wind up on couches, talking to those with psychology degrees about inkblot butterflies resembling female body parts.

I didn't make it long in the medical profession; however, the bird's-eye view did serve to teach a few invaluable life lessons. First, your thighs matter. No need to elaborate on how I came to said revelation, but then and there I decided life was too short for flabby thighs. It was my own personal #BeTheChange moment, and I could have kissed Suzanne Somers and her ThighMaster for having already conquered that Everest.

I'm guessing my parents considered my summer internship a bust when I was demoted to the back room for filing papers, but I choose to think of it as that season when I perfected my ThighMaster technique. Which brings me to my second life lesson: muscle memory works.

Even though the ThighMaster recommended fifteen to twenty minutes a day for fab thighs, I had ample time in the filing room to give it a good five to six hours a day. I'm here to tell you, I experienced a miraculous toning that summer, and I'd give up my firstborn to get it back. (As an aside, I'm not even sure muscle memory was the "science" behind this $300 million invention, but just go with it because we've already established that I'm no medical professional.)

I've found that muscle memory is a key component of both fitness and our faith. The idea is to commit specific motor tasks to memory by doing them over and over again.[1] Applying muscle memory to faith is training ourselves to operate in a way that honors God without having to concentrate on it every time. Said differently, we're working to make things so routine in our prayer life or Bible study or faith walk that it becomes second nature to do things as God calls us to when life throws a curveball.

Muscle memory plays a big part in hearing God speak. We make it super complicated when it comes to hearing from God, thinking we've got to be in the right place geographically or, even more so, spiritually for it to happen. That all the stars have to align with a choir singing "A Mighty Fortress Is Our God" before we're assured we've received a word from God.

But I've learned we're actually born with the muscle memory it takes to hear God's voice. I saw a glimpse of it when our daughter was born. She was just minutes into her little life and crying like crazy in the delivery room as the nurses checked her out. My husband gently called her name from across the room and reassured her that it was okay. Instantly she stopped crying and turned her head in his direction.

A nurse commented on how miraculous it is that from the moment they're born, the tiniest of babies recognizes their parents' voices. I guess it made sense, considering Kate had been listening to her dad talk to her for months in the womb. (No, we didn't have one of those freaky microphone and headphone setups for him to talk through my belly. Let's be serious here.)

But even in the craziness of the delivery room, with lights and doctors and nurses and the shock of having been forced onto planet earth, her father's voice was unmistakable.

And so it is with our heavenly Father.

Since the very moment we were formed in our mother's womb, God has been speaking to us. He lovingly calls us by name and rejoices over us with singing. And just as Kate intuitively knew her father's voice in the chaos of the operating room, we are conditioned to hear God's voice. It's in our DNA.

The enemy wants us to believe we're not important enough or spiritual enough or forgiven enough to receive a word from the God of the universe. That's for other, more "spiritual" people. Nothing could be less true. It's just that, as the world gets busier and noisier and harder, it takes a little more intentionality to hear His still, small voice in our everyday lives.

That's where muscle memory comes into play. Just as the ThighMaster works best with repetition, hearing God speak into our everyday lives takes regular and consistent practice. The more you do it, the better you become at it. (You can thank me later, as I'm guessing there's no seminary in the world suggesting the ThighMaster is similar to hearing God's voice.)

It starts by positioning ourselves to hear from God. Just as tiny Kate turned her head to hear Mike's voice, we can turn ours by tuning out Netflix, Instagram, Spotify, our phones, and anything else that brings noise when we most need quiet. That's the beginning of getting down to the business of listening for God, who calls each of us individually and speaks to us personally.

> *What would you do, or not do, if you knew God was going to speak to you today?*

But even aside from quieting ourselves to hear from God, we've got to train ourselves with a sense of expectation to hear His voice. A. W. Tozer says, "It is the nature of God to speak."[2] Literally, it's who He is, and He created us to listen.

When day after day and week after week we posture ourselves to hear from God while also living in expectation of hearing His voice, we're putting in the muscle memory for a life that's filled with God-ordained moments of clarity, purpose, and community.

Knowing this, I wonder how different our lives would be if we lived each day expecting to hear from God.

What would you do, or not do, if you knew God was going to speak to you today? What would you ask Him about? How would you pray differently?

How would the people around you be changed if you allowed God to speak into everything you have planned for the next seventy-two hours?

COURT HEARINGS AND HEARING GOD

The discipline to hear God's voice was the game changer in Pastor Pierre's life. He never articulated that, but it was evident in his actions: the way he drove across town during the busiest time of year to pray for a family he had never even met, praying outside our home and waiting for God to respond, and then boldly sharing the words with us.

This wasn't the first time he had experienced God's voice in a bold and clear way, that was obvious. He wasn't hemming and haw-ing like I might have with a somewhat apologetic, "I think maybe God was saying the hearing will be fine," or "Don't quote me on this, but I think God's going to do something cool tomorrow, but we should pray anyway."

No, he heard God's voice—the same one he obviously had heard countless times before—and he spoke boldly in a house full of people who needed a reminder that God has power and authority over *all* things.

Let's be clear, the outcome of JB's hearing would not have changed if Pastor Pierre had stayed home that night to work on his Christmas Eve sermon; God's plan was God's plan. But in hearing God's voice, we were given the much-needed reminder that God is sovereign over all things, and not for one day has He been limited by court systems, judges, or legal processes. Every day of JB's life was already written in His book before even one came to pass, and a little hearing in a Dallas County courtroom the next day had little bearing on it—because nothing is left to chance with God.

Nothing.

I found out later Pastor Pierre went home that night and relayed to his wife the happenings and his words about the hearing the next day. Apparently she said, "You said what? What if you're wrong?" I can appreciate her sentiment, because I had that same thought for a split second when CPS called twelve hours later.

But just as the Lord said through Pastor Pierre the evening before, the judge ruled that JB was ours to adopt. And against all odds, this little boy became a Yanof shortly thereafter.

As for Pastor Pierre, I've only seen him one other time since that night, but he will forever hold a sweet place in JB's story and our hearts. I'm betting he would want me to mention how today is a fresh opportunity to find quiet in the middle of the chaos, to turn our heads toward our Father, and to wait expectantly for the God of the universe to speak into our lives.

CHAPTER 13

Writing a Book Nobody Will Read

MESSY TRUTH

I pray we never buy into the lie that the seemingly ordinary things are not good enough and that doing the things nobody else will ever see is insignificant.

A few years ago, Mike decided to write a book. My husband's the kind of guy who decides to do something, and then just sits down and does it. There wasn't a lot of fanfare or hype around his decision. He didn't ask us to plan a fancy kickoff dinner or gather our friends to garner support. He didn't even ask to redecorate our home office or plan a few writing retreats in cool locations as part of his preparations. (I mean, who would need to do that, right?)

He just woke up super early every single morning, hours before he needed to go to work, and methodically cranked out a book at our kitchen counter. He wrote about the ways God had been pursuing him for as long as he could remember, through ordinary things like family vacations, playing college baseball, getting married, and doing life as both a lawyer and a parent.

He even wrote a chapter about a few guys he played baseball with in high school. They were your typical jock-type guys, but they also lived differently because they knew Jesus. He didn't know what it was about these guys that drew him in, but on a quest to figure it out, Mike accepted their invitation to a Fellowship of Christian Athletes (FCA) breakfast. And it was through FCA that Mike was introduced to the Bible and eventually became a Christian—all because of a few teenage guys who encountered Jesus and lived differently because of it. (That will preach.)

After months of writing, Mike finished his book and started down the road to getting it published. Neither of us had a clue about the publishing world at the time, so Mike did a few Google searches and began sending his manuscript to literary agents in hopes of finding a publisher. Unfortunately, he hit brick wall after brick wall and had no success in getting an agent or securing a publisher.

Mike wasn't really bitter or upset about how it played out; he's super humble that way. He doesn't place expectations on people or assume motives in the face of rejection. He just casually mentioned to me that it seems that *ordinary doesn't sell* because, understandably, most people aren't interested in the stories of an everyday guy who, for the most part, has lived a pretty regular life.

LIES OUR CULTURE TELLS

Several years ago, I came across an article written by David Brooks, a political and cultural commentator for the *New York Times*, among other titles he holds. He's also written several books that have appeared on various bestseller lists, so that's definitely something. The topic that caught my attention: "Five Lies Our Culture Tells."

His article addressed our country's devastating suicide rates, our overflowing mental health facilities, and the divisive political issues that (in his opinion) all boil down to one root problem: our culture is built on lies.

These are some of the false premises he believes are devastating our culture:

> *Career success is fulfilling.* He believes we engrain this in our kids through a higher education system that preaches "if you make it, you will be good."

I can make myself happy. The belief that self-sufficiency or individual accomplishment brings us happiness.

Life is an individual journey. Following this tempts us to stay unattached and on the move because the person with the most experiences wins.

You have to find your own truth. Everyone is uniquely and individually responsible for finding their own values and answering life's ultimate questions.

Rich and successful people are worth more than poorer and less successful people. We may vehemently deny this message, yet it's rooted in a meritocracy that says "you are what you accomplish."[1]

The lies David Brooks identifies instantly resonated with me, even as my faith informs my reasoning as to why they are so damaging. It's hard to argue he's off base considering we live in a world that says we need to *have more, do more,* and *be more* in order to be valued. That success is the highest goal, yet the measure of success is constantly being redefined.

I was reminded how I've spent a hot minute (or two or three) tangled up in these lies myself, defining success by the size of my clothes, the square footage of my house, and the size of my wallet. Heck, I've even measured my worth by the accolades my kids receive, the career path of my spouse, and (especially problematic) the acknowledgment of my peers.

But when our worth is contingent on how successful we become or how exceptional our life turns out—with "making it" being the highest of goals—then anything short of that begins to feel unsuccessful or mediocre or even worse yet ... ordinary.

WHAT THE WORLD CALLS ORDINARY

Once Mike realized his book was headed down a one-way road to nowhere, he decided to take it to a local print shop and have some copies made for posterity's sake. I'm guessing that after all those months of writing a book, it probably felt like a give-up, being reduced to a makeshift printer with none of the commercial appeal of cool cover art or fancy typeface or even endorsements and forewords to set the tone for the book.

It was early December, so Mike threw a few copies into gift bags to give his parents and me for Christmas. A couple weeks later, in the middle of our Christmas morning craziness, I opened my copy of the book. I'll never forget how Mike, somewhat apologetically, downplayed the book's significance. He was quick to make sure I knew this wasn't *the* gift he was giving me, but just a little something extra he had thrown in that was no big deal.

But what Mike grossly underestimated that Christmas morning was how this simple, unassuming, and *unpublishable* book has been the very best gift he's ever given our family.

It's true, Mike's life has been pretty ordinary for the most part. He went to school, got married, started a career, and set his sights on raising kids, loving his wife, and supporting his family. He hasn't traveled the world or amassed a fortune or gained notoriety that gets him noticed in restaurants or gifted box seats to the hottest sporting events.

But behind the ordinary, we've been given a front row seat to watching him choose a minute-by-minute, hour-by-hour, and day-by-day life that honors his family and, more importantly, his faith. We've seen that what the world calls ordinary, his friends call reliable. What the world calls ordinary, his colleagues call reputable. What the world calls ordinary, his kids call dependable. What the world calls ordinary, his wife calls faithful. And what the world calls ordinary, the Lord calls holy.

I've watched him walk away from corner-office jobs and career-advancing opportunities because he knows *career success is not fulfilling*. He's fought back against the idea that *I can make myself happy* or *life is an individual journey* because he cares far more about our souls than his status.

When it comes to *finding your own truth*, he knows the only real truth is found in Jesus—and so he points us in that direction daily. And if our culture really does believe that *poorer and less successful people are worth less than others* (please let this not be true), he's fought back by living a life marked by foster care and ministry.

That being said, I'm guessing there have been moments when Mike has probably wished for something more. I'm sure he would have loved to write a *New York Times*–bestselling book or even to have a David Brooks'–type article picked up by a prestigious publication. He's surely wished for a little more recognition, acclaim, acknowledgment, and appreciation. I mean, who wouldn't?

But my prayer is for him to see that the story he's writing through his everyday life is of *far greater value* than the brief shelf life of a commercially published book (mine included) or a thousand-word op-ed landing in a Sunday edition of a newspaper.

And the same goes for us.

Right there in the middle of our everyday life of changing diapers, carpooling to soccer, and gathering our expense receipts is where God is using our ordinary, unpublishable lives to do mighty things that will change the trajectory of those around us.

Can I be honest here for a minute? (That's rhetorical; I'm going there.) In a culture built on lies, we've got to fight harder than ever to build lives on truth. It reminds me of a Bible passage where Jesus warns us not to build our houses on sand because the storms will come and our houses will fall apart if there's no firm foundation holding it together (Matt. 7:24–27). Instead, He says to build our houses on rock, because no matter what the trials of life bring our way, our foundation is solid and our houses can withstand the storm.

Building a house on sand, very plainly, is building it on the lies in our culture instead of on the truths of Jesus. I don't know if you struggle with the lies David Brooks identifies—or other lies based in identity and self-sufficiency, like I do. But the one lie I pray we will never buy into is that ordinary is not good enough. That doing the right things—the honorable things, the hard things, and the things that nobody will ever see or acknowledge—is insignificant. Because believing that lie is building a house on sandy ground.

Jesus is in the business of using everything in our lives—even the painful, ordinary, and unpublishable chapters—for extraordinary purposes in His larger kingdom.

Just recently, Mike and I were given the privilege of paying an ungodly amount of money to have our landscaping destroyed while also repairing the foundation of our home. It was super fun dropping two Disney trips' worth of cash on something that nobody will ever notice. To this day, not one person has come by our house commenting, "Nice foundation," or "Way to flex all those new piers."

Nobody has noticed.

Nobody cares.

And we've received not one single "attaboy" for having fixed an otherwise shaky foundation.

But that lack of recognition doesn't change the fact that our foundation was and still is the most critical part of our house. It's the very thing that keeps it standing. And all the pretty window treatments and new furniture and beautifully stained hardwood floors (and nice cars and exotic vacations and athletic kids) in the world won't matter if our foundation isn't built on "the rock" of Jesus. Can I get an amen? (Not rhetorical this time.)

Because when the foundation company came and lifted our house, it took not one or three or five piers and pillars to put us back on solid ground; it took sixteen.

I'm left wondering how many pillars we need to drill down into the bedrock of God's Word in order to be raised to His higher ground.

- Parenting pillars that say no when everyone else is saying yes
- Generosity pillars that give extravagantly instead of living excessively

- Humility pillars that say little when you are entitled to say much
- Marriage pillars that lean in when you'd rather walk out
- Loyalty pillars that shut down conversations when you're tempted to chime in
- Faith pillars that trust God's hand instead of trying your own
- Contentment pillars that stay home when you'd rather be seen out
- Perspective pillars that believe God uses the small things to accomplish His mighty purposes

Don't be deceived; these pillars don't often bring earthly accolades or applause. Nobody will walk past your metaphorical house and comment, "Hey, nice pillars you've put into place for building a life based on truth instead of lies."

But living a life that's built on rock—embracing what may seem painfully ordinary and refusing to buy into the lies our culture is selling about success and worth—allows God to take our temporary lives and use them for eternal impact.

ORDINARY EVENTS MADE EXTRAORDINARY

A few days ago, as I was finishing this chapter, I pulled out Mike's book because I couldn't remember the title. I laughed out loud when

I saw that it was *Ordinary Events Made Extraordinary*, because that's literally where I prayed this chapter would land.

I want to make it clear that Mike is anything but ordinary to those who know and love him. He's successful not only by the world's standards but more importantly by God's standards. Yet if you're anything like me, you need reminders that Jesus is in the business of using everything in our lives—even the painful, ordinary, and unpublishable chapters—for extraordinary purposes in His larger kingdom.

And I don't know who needs to hear this today, but in a world that says you must be more, do more, and have more to prove your worth, please give yourself permission to lean into the ordinary. Millions of books will tell you to chase your dreams, live your best life, or accept nothing short of an accomplished life, but may this be the one that challenges you to define your version of success by first lining it up with God's.

Long before our physical house needed foundation work, my husband was already busy putting his own pillars in place. These pillars of faith have secured our family on the bedrock of Christ, and that's in large part because of his willingness to live a steady and unassuming life. And all the while, the Author of all creation has been faithfully taking the ordinary and using it for extraordinary things that aren't always measurable on this side of heaven.

I can think of no better way to wrap this up than to leave you with a quote from one of the greatest books you'll never read:

> When faith defines us, hope sustains us, and love
> motivates us, the lens through which we see life is

different. We come to care about the things God cares about. We ask him to guide us in what he'd have us do. And my experience is, when we live this way, otherwise ordinary lives and experiences are transformed into the extraordinary.[2]

Mike Yanof,
Ordinary Events Made Extraordinary

CHAPTER 14

I'm Sorry?

MESSY TRUTH

The journey of forgiveness is less about our heart
for those who wronged us, and more about our
heart toward the One who relentlessly forgives us.

We realized our daughter was "gifted" in about sixth grade. It was right around her thirteenth birthday when we woke up one day to find she was above average in the category of middle-school girl hideousness. I know that may seem harsh, especially if you haven't parented middle school girls. But if you have, then I'm just articulating what you've been secretly thinking, and I'm guessing you could write your own chapter on this topic.

How would I describe these years?

It's living with a Lululemon-wearing, AirPods-listening, long-hair-straightening terrorist of sorts. Your days are filled with the hijacking of family meals, hostage-style negotiations through bathroom doors, and cyberattacks of the worst kind—selfies. The climate of fear is real enough to make one shudder at the thought of suggesting the need to tidy her room or, worse yet, pull down her microscopic shorts in order to better cover her unmentionables.

One of the most unique attributes of this middle school preciousness is a belief system based on being smarter than everyone else on the planet—especially those over the age of twenty (who are not influencers, duh). Never mind one's parents have successfully navigated grade school, completed college, earned two law degrees, held down jobs, paid for the home in which she literally resides ... all irrelevant. It's meaningless because we're old and outdated and completely out of touch.

You just don't get it. (Truth, we really do not get it.)

Being adults and everything, Mike and I continued to parent and feed her because the law required it of us. But we also held out hope that one day she would mysteriously snap out of it as fast as she'd caught it. And thankfully, in just a few months—albeit long and tedious months—this crossbreed between a cactus and a feral cat returned to being our lovely daughter.

Of course, along the way we loved her, disciplined her, and even expected her to apologize when she crossed the line with her notorious eye rolls and hair flips. And to her credit, Kate was always quick to apologize. But sadly, even her very words of apology were like nails on a chalkboard to me. Until I figured out why.

After a particularly long weekend of snarkiness, I got on Kate for something I can't even remember. She responded with her typical apology of "I'm sorry?" And at that moment I realized why her apologetic utterances were pushing me over the ledge: she was apologizing in the form of a question. *I'm sorry?*

Try it for yourself. The next time a frenemy gets all riled up at you, give them your best thirteen-year-old girl response: *I'm sorry?* They will simultaneously appreciate the words while wondering why they find you more annoying than ever.

The problem with apologizing in the form of a question is while the words are right, the heart is not.

THE HARDEST CHAPTER YOU'LL WRITE

After fifty trips around the sun, I realize there have been many times I've needed to give a heartfelt "I'm sorry." Sometimes I've done it well, and other times not so much. I like to think as I've aged, I've gotten better at apologizing. But I also know that many times my apologies, like Kate's, have come in the form of a question because my words were right but my heart was not.

Waiting on the other side of every apology is God's call for us to respond in forgiveness. I think the hardest places of forgiveness I've faced are those where no apology has been offered or, even worse, I've been offered an apology of "I'm sorry?"

I'm willing to confess that I've struggled with forgiveness at times in my life. So much so that I've put off writing this chapter until the absolute last second before this book's deadline. Yet, as difficult as a chapter on unforgiveness is to write, it's an even harder chapter to walk.

I wish there was a perfect formula or five-step plan for mastering forgiveness. If only it were so simple. Are there some small places where we might need to get over ourselves and let it go? Probably. Do we hang on to small things that barely matter in the name of being right? Absolutely. The moral high ground is a dangerously pious place if we aren't careful.

But what about forgiveness in those really deep, hard places where the hurt is painfully raw and trite words anchored in smart colloquialisms will never be enough? I assure you I can relate, and only recently have I resurfaced from a very personal season of hurt, confusion, and feeling grossly misunderstood.

As I find myself finally coming up for air, I appreciate how the journey to forgiveness is sometimes (oftentimes) slow, personal, and methodical. I've also learned forgiveness is less about our heart for those who wronged us and more about our heart toward the One who loves and forgives us.

My road to forgiveness has similarities to the story of Jonah. God told him to go and preach words of life to his most bitter enemies, and Jonah was like "Ummm ... you got the wrong guy

The sting of betrayal eludes forgiveness when our salvation has a seat anywhere other than in the nail-scarred hands of our Savior.

here." He told Jonah to go east, and Jonah hightailed it to the west. Jonah had zero interest in being the vessel of deliverance for the Ninevites. So much so that he asked a bunch of sailors to throw him off a ship on the way to Tarshish because death felt better than obedience if it meant compassion and kindness toward his greatest enemies.

But in His mercy, God didn't leave Jonah to die alone in the murky waters of disobedience. He gave him some time to reflect in the belly of a whale, knowing eventually (I mean e-ven-tu-al-ly) Jonah would come around. And Jonah did come to his senses in a kinda, sorta, half-witting way and apologized for his actions without ever saying actual words of apology.

God responded to his "I'm sorry?" with vomit (I can appreciate that) and sent him packing to Nineveh with a sour spirit but a saving message. Ironically, the message Jonah so adamantly didn't want to deliver to the Ninevites is the same five words I've found to be a key to forgiveness:

Salvation comes from the LORD. (Jon. 2:9)

Sure, at first glance those words seem like nicey-nice church words filling lofty airspace and don't speak to our deepest hurts. But stay with me for a minute. If salvation *only comes from the Lord*, why have we been looking for it somewhere else?

Merriam-Webster defines *salvation* as "preservation from destruction or failure."[1] It's the thing(s) we cling to in a tumultuous world full of unknowns. I've sought salvation (and worth, and contentment, and significance) in my work, my spouse, my finances, my performance, and my status, to name only a few. And when those things inevitably fail me, my destruction feels real and my self-preservation kicks in, leaving me bitter, angry, and, yes, unforgiving.

That's what happens when we allow the things of this life to take root where God never created them to reside. Deep pain results in a long road of recovery and forgiveness.

Yes, friends have wronged me or failed to defend me—but God never created them to shelter me.

Yes, my work has left me hurt and betrayed—but God never intended my work to fulfill me.

Yes, my marriage has been hard some days, and my husband isn't perfect—but God never created him to complete me.

Only when I surrender these things—and claim Jesus as my *only* salvation—can I find a path to forgiveness and peace in the deepest hurt I've faced. Jesus alone forgives us unconditionally. He alone is our hope. He alone is our shield. He alone is our defender. He alone is our provider. He alone is enough.

Not Jesus + someone's approval
Not Jesus + my spouse
Not Jesus + my kids' accolades
Not Jesus + my friends' loyalty
Not Jesus + my health
Not Jesus + my safety
Not Jesus + __(fill in the blank)__

It's sticky business giving the wrong priority to otherwise right relationships. The sting of betrayal eludes forgiveness when our salvation has a seat anywhere other than in the nail-scarred hands of our Savior.

So, like you, I've walked through some hard places where I *knew* God was calling me to forgive someone or something. One of those places is still painfully fresh. Most days I've wanted to flee to Tarshish instead of walking in obedience to Nineveh.

But trusting God as your only salvation means holding loosely to those things that will inevitably let you down. And by loosening your grip, you're knocking down the walls to forgiveness and grace—no longer holding people to a standard they can't deliver on.

In Lysa TerKeurst's book, *Forgiving What You Can't Forget*, she says:

> The more our pain consumes us, the more it will control us. And sadly, it's those who least deserve to be hurt whom our unresolved pain will hurt the most. That person or people—they've caused enough pain for you, for me, and for those around us. They've taken enough. You get to decide how you'll move forward.[2]

To be clear, I'm in no way trying to downplay the hard roads we've walked. These places are not made up or situations where we've been too sensitive. But I've found that waiting for an earnest apology is giving power to the one who wronged me, instead of laying it down before the only One who can save me.

SOMETHING'S DRAGGING BEHIND YOU

At the risk of diving into awkwardly shallow water as I wrap up a rather deep topic, I'm going to share my mom's most embarrassing moment from high school. She was getting ready for prom and doing all the things you do for the most important night of your life.

She had her makeup done. She had her hair fixed. She had shopped with her mom and found a beautiful dress for this important occasion. To top it all off, she had the most amazing date, a cute and popular boy who had noticed her in a sea of girls and asked her to prom.

So after hours of preparing for the big night, she came out of her room in her full-length dress covered in delicate lace. She went to her parents' bedroom to look at herself in the full-length mirror, admire her beautiful dress, and put finishing touches on her hair. Moments later her date arrived, and she left her parents' room and walked down the hall to greet him.

After pleasantries were spoken and flowers exchanged, my mom and her date headed out for an evening they would never forget. Or at least she wouldn't. As her date was opening her car door, she noticed him awkwardly pausing as if there was something he was reluctantly trying to say. Finally, he got up the nerve to sheepishly let my mom know there was something dragging behind her dress.

My mother looked down and was horrified. When she had gone into her parents' bedroom moments before her date arrived, the clasp of her mother's size 44D bra had caught the lace on the back of her dress. And this extra-large bra was trailing behind my mom and her date as they headed off for the dance.

May I be the one to sheepishly and reluctantly mention that you may be dragging a little something too? A lifetime of unforgiveness isn't exactly dragging around your mother's embarrassingly big bra, but it's visible to others even if we can't see it ourselves.

Forgive freely by clinging to Jesus, and place your salvation in Him alone.

And if I've offended you or have been too blunt in discussing forgiveness, *I'm sorry?*

CHAPTER 15

Playground Rules

MESSY TRUTH

The playground is full of great reminders that our best parenting lives at the intersection of imparting necessary life skills while refusing to obsess over the millions of things that just don't matter.

I don't mind a good trip to the playground on occasion. The smelly zoo? I'll pass. The Band-Aid–floating, hairball-ridden water parks? Surely you jest; that's what husbands are for, after all.

But I do frequent the local parks on occasion, which deserves a round of applause now that I'm middle-aged (assuming one lives to one hundred) and managing a small child once again. A few years ago, I was at the park in hopes of a little energy burn for my youngest, and it hit me how many parenting truths come from simply watching playground protocol.

As I sat there watching these younger moms sliding the slides, swinging the swings, and doing all the things with their kids (while, naturally, I scrolled Instagram), I was reminded of my own days as a young mom. I desperately wondered what *really* mattered in raising kids. As much as I wanted to be sure our family was about the right and significant things, I very practically wondered what those things actually were.

Now that I'm twenty years down the road of being a mom, I realize there are some playground rules I wish someone would have mentioned to me earlier. The truth is, I probably wouldn't have heard them then. Some things only make sense once you're the most "senior" (not senior citizen) mom on the playground. That said, here are some playground-turned-parenting rules I wish I had known.

Playground Rule #1
THERE'S PLENTY OF ROOM FOR EVERYONE

One of the great things about the playground is there's no gate-keeper. Nobody stands at the proverbial entrance with a checklist of questions deciding who is a fit for the playground and who is not. You'll never hear things like:

> *Whoa, ma'am, let's slow the wagon down until we decide if your little bundle is headed to public or private school in a few years.*

> *You in the fanny pack over there, did you bottle or breastfeed?*

> *Parents of the wild kid spitting on the picnic table, this is a time-out-only park, so please no spanking.*

Life is simple at the playground because there are no qualifications for inclusion. Your kids don't have to be "gifted" to play tag. You don't have to be politically aligned to push the swings. Everyone is accepted at the playground. Everyone has a place. Everyone is welcome.

But somewhere outside the playground paradigm, we institute a parenting funneling system of sorts. It starts off as a wide funnel where we're all doing life together as young married types, having babies, going to parenting classes, and showing up at the baby showers. But then, as our kids get a little bit further down the road, we start funneling in or limiting who we're going to do life with based on what we've decided is the "right" way to do things.

We distance ourselves from people based on how they discipline or where they live or the school their kids attend or even what sports teams their kids do or don't make. We make judgments based on social media posts, friend groups, and even decisions other kids make that we don't agree with for our own.

We funnel down so narrowly that one day we wake up surrounded only by those who parent exactly how we do, or at least by how we have deemed the right way to raise kids. We have little margin for those walking a different path because we've surrounded ourselves with people who are mirrors of how we think, how we look, and who say the things we want to hear.

Fact: *One of the kindest things we can do is simply include others.*

I wish I would have known sooner that commonality isn't a critical factor to doing life with those around us. Just as I saw on the playground all those years ago, there's room enough for everyone on our parenting journey. We don't have to change people to walk alongside them, and we're not endorsing them by loving them. It's not compromising to include people, and we don't have to fix them to be a friend to them.

Now I know someone is reading this and thinking, *But there really are some people I don't want my kids hanging around.* I can appreciate this because I'm raising one of those kids! Having grown up in a world of teenagers, my youngest knows way too much about Bruno Mars and high school romances for any good mom's sensibilities. Even so, it's hard to be salt and light when we live a life that's separated and legalistic.

Loving people well is sometimes as simple as making a place for everyone at our table. It's a willingness to clear our crazy schedules and create margin for others. It's getting comfortable with being uncomfortable in order to widen our circle and bring others in.

I've realized I can't raise kids who are willing to be vulnerable and enter into other people's messes if I'm not willing to do it myself. It's nudging them to invite others even when it's not popular. It's teaching them to see the needs around them and be relentless in finding ways to meet them. It's refusing to make our world so small that only a select few people can ever fit within the parameters of it.

Like it or not, my family will be known for something. I hope it's for making room for everyone.

Playground Rule #2
DON'T SWEAT SLIDE ETIQUETTE

This same day at the park, I noticed a little boy who was determined to climb up the front side of the slide rather than using the stairs to then slide down. His mom wasn't having it, and over and over again she corrected him by pulling him off the slide and relocating him to the stairs.

I mean no disrespect to this conscientious mom clearly trying to train up a respectful son who plays by the rules; however, I was reminded of how many parenting hills I've died on because I've bought into the lie that there's only one way to get to the top.

Fact: *There is more than one way to the top, and we should celebrate our kids as they find their unique way of getting there.*

The notion that there's only one "right" way to do things is fairly ridiculous when we consider that God created each of our children uniquely. Not a one of them is designed exactly like another. Yet we oftentimes find ourselves with a level of expectation that requires our kids to be perfect students (in all subjects), amazing athletes, resourceful citizens, outgoing teens, motivated go-getters, and, if all goes well, class favorite and homecoming queen.

Were you all those things growing up? I surely was not.

Let's chalk up my younger self to being a mediocre student who was ridiculously unathletic and 100 percent unremarkable by today's standards. Yet God, over and over again, uses normal, seemingly unqualified people for significance by leading them to higher ground using His path, not the world's.

Who is with me?

So many of our kids will take a different path, and that's okay. Your kids may be in the less-popular friend group or lower math class; they may develop slower or, God forbid, be in the marching band! (I can say this because I marched and have the sad plume and shiny shoes to prove it.) That's to be expected from a God who calls His unique kids to unique roads leading down the perfect path to Him.

Look around and consider how many of our most successful adults have gotten where they are by swimming upstream and walking the road less traveled. They are creative, out-of-the-box thinkers who march to the beat of their own drums. They probably looked like failures long before there was even the slightest hint of success.

Albert Einstein didn't speak a word until he was four, and Walt Disney was fired from a newspaper for a lack of creativity. Elvis Presley was rejected from a vocal quartet because he couldn't sing,

The notion that there's only one "right" way to do things is fairly ridiculous when we consider that God created each of our children uniquely.

and Thomas Edison had thousands of creative misses before finally inventing the light bulb.[1]

The playground is a great reminder that good parenting lives at the intersection of imparting necessary life skills while refusing to obsess over the millions of things that just don't matter in the long run. It's parenting the bigger picture of character while letting go of the messy bedrooms, strict bedtimes, matching clothes, perfect grades, and over-the-top expectations that don't further God's bigger plans.

There are a lot of ways to get to the top, and we have the opportunity each day to celebrate our kids' unique path of getting there. Take it from Thomas Edison, who said it this way: "I have not failed. I've just found 10,000 ways that won't work."[2]

Playground Rule #3
IT'S OKAY TO PLAY ALONE

Nothing raises our parenting hackles more than finding our kids playing alone in the middle of a packed playground (or, really, any social situation). It takes every bit of our willpower not to march right out there and socially engineer the heck out of that failed bit for fear of producing the next social outcast.

Let's be honest, we're all just one bad playground outing away from reliving every single one of our junior high insecurities. I wasn't invited to the cool kid's thirteenth birthday party and neither were you, and yes, I mistakenly wore my orthodontic headgear to the popular girls' sleepover and, all things considered, we're still okay.

Fact: *If we want kids who can stand alone in today's culture, we've got to let them.*

We're raising kids in a culture that is divided politically, economically, racially, financially (and probably any other "-lly" word you can think of). I've realized if our kids are going to live out their faith and do the things God has uniquely called them to do, they need to be willing and able to do it alone sometimes.

I remember seeing a picture on social media years ago for one of those "See You at the Pole" days when Christian kids all over the country gather at their schools' flagpoles to pray. The picture posted by this mom showed her son at the flagpole with his Bible in hand, praying completely alone while masses of students walked past him in the background.

I was moved by the picture and remember thinking, *I want to raise this kind of kid.* I want to raise kids who are so committed to following God, they are willing to get up, shut up, show up, and speak up for what's right even when no one else around them does. I want kids who have the fortitude to walk the right path even when it's the unpopular one, and the character and conviction to do what's right even if it means doing it completely alone.

But allowing our kids to play alone takes some significant restraint on our part. It means refusing to march down to the school every time our kid doesn't get in the "right" class or make the "right" team or receive the "right" accolade. It's being okay when they don't get invited to the party, and not planning an even bigger one to "show them" for not including your baby (let's not act like we've never considered doing this, all right?). It's flipping the script in the places where it feels like our kids are being punished, choosing instead to see it as provision, knowing they will come out stronger on the other side.

And then there's the whole thing of needing to actually model it for our kids by being willing to stand alone in our own lives. Who knew it was going to be so hard even as adults? I can think of so many times when I should have walked away from a conversation or looked away from a text string or stayed away from the group that was *really, really* fun but *really, really* not what I'm about. I've learned the call to stand alone doesn't just apply to our kids.

The playground has taught me it's okay for my kids to be alone as they play at the park or after school on Friday or on the bench during the biggest soccer game of the season—because allowing our kids to walk alone *today* is the best way to teach them how to do it well *tomorrow*.

Playground Rule #4
DON'T THROW WOOD CHIPS

As I was leaving the playground that day, I saw a little boy picking up wood chips off the ground and throwing them. The other kids took note and also began throwing wood chips at each other until it was basically wood-chip anarchy. A mom (probably a beloved teacher) finally stepped in and yelled, "Everyone stop throwing wood chips!" And they did.

Fact: *Kids aren't the only ones who throw wood chips.*

I've learned firsthand that sometimes in parenthood we need someone willing to bring a stop to all the wood-chip throwing. I've said it before and I'll say it again: nothing brings out our inner-sanctimoniousness like having kids. We become so judgment prone that we're willing to speak into hard places we've actually never had to walk. We throw wood chips that look like gossipy phone calls after playdates, eye rolls across the room at school functions, and "prayer requests" for kids who have chosen hard and undesirable paths.

I say it because I've done it.

We teach our kids very early on that hurling wood chips at other people is unkind and not allowed. But we sometimes forget it later in life. The playground has taught me the importance of being the one willing to end the cruel conversation or say a kind word to the struggling mom or invite the "different" kid over. It's giving grace and space for people to be imperfect by putting down the wood chips and picking up some compassion for those trying as hard as we are to get it right.

These are but a few of the parenting truths I've learned over the years. But thankfully, God continues to gracefully and consistently remind me to make room for others, put down the wood chips, and allow my kids to take their own unique paths toward their Creator, even if sometimes it means doing it alone.

As it turns out, the playground is the perfect training ground for many of life's greatest lessons—both for our kids and their parents.

CHAPTER 16

A Ghost Story

MESSY TRUTH

In a world questioning the realness of God
more and more with each passing year, it's never
been more critical for us to make sure our *why*
matches up with the why of the gospel.

*L*ast summer we went to Boston for our family vacation. Look at you, Boston, all fabulous with your historical landmarks, picturesque water views, top-notch colleges, and, of course, the duck boats.

We fell in love with walking the Freedom Trail and learning American history we probably should have already known. We ate lobster rolls and clam chowder followed by cannoli, which have forever changed my life (and waistline). We even went to the aquarium and pretended to be interested in aquamarine life for half a day, all in the name of doing just one thing our six-year-old might enjoy.

There was Fenway Park and the "green monster," which was a bucket list item for my husband, who dreams of touring the Major League Baseball stadiums. We wrapped it all up with the Fourth of July fireworks spectacular and the Boston symphony. It was the perfect cherry on the top before we headed home with full hearts and COVID coughs.

But knowing no vacation is perfect, it's with full transparency I mention just one minor-ish incident.

We went on a ghost tour.

Well, let me back up a bit.

It should have been enough that my people were thoroughly enjoying themselves in Boston. They were perfectly happy doing all the Boston things when I insisted we take an excursion to Salem, Massachusetts, for a ghost tour. Now I know what you're probably thinking, so let me explain before you judge my ghost tour (and then you will still judge, but I'll at least feel better about it).

When Mike and I graduated from law school, my parents took us to Washington, DC, and then Williamsburg, Virginia, for a few days. We loved Williamsburg, and one of our favorite memories was a quaint little ghost tour. Picture people dressed in 1700s attire, holding their darling little lanterns. There were cobblestone streets and ghost stories told over cups of hot cocoa. It couldn't have been more charming.

So with this particular picture in my head, we loaded up the rental car and headed sixteen miles north to Salem to relive our best ghost tour memories with our kids. Now perhaps the fact that we struggled to find a "kid-friendly tour" online should have been my first clue— not to mention the Salem witch trials and all that business—but my mind was made up, and I'm not one to be easily deterred.

Once we arrived in Salem, it didn't take long for me to figure out the two critical facts: (1) Salem is not exactly Williamsburg, and (2) all ghost tours are not created equal.

The second clue came as our soon-to-be tour guide showed up in her own style of period clothing, which was a far cry from the Williamsburg attire and more like Holly Hobbie prepares for front-line combat. It was a journey.

She began the tour with what I naively believed to be a rhetorical question: "Who here believes in ghosts?" I assumed this was a cutesy little "who believes in Casper" kind of thing, meant to hype up the kids, like listening for reindeer hooves on the roof on Christmas Eve. But I soon realized I was way off when every single person on the tour raised a hand. Every. Single. Person.

Well, every single person minus the five Yanofs.

Even as I was sensing things might be a little off, I felt a glimmer of hope when Holly Hobbie began laying out some ground rules for the next few hours. No cursing. No smoking. And no vaping because, after all, this was a kid-friendly tour. But about ten minutes in, as she launched into the story of a soldier from the 1800s who was mutilated in front of stop #2, I realized there may have been a slight misjudgment on my part.

I glanced over at my family just in time to see my youngest mesmerized by stories of the soldier who could still be heard gasping for air and screaming out at night as he haunts people. And to add insult to injury, Kate (in her most sarcastic, nineteen-year-old voice) said, "Thank goodness nobody is allowed to smoke or cuss on this super *kid-friendly* tour, Mom. We sure wouldn't want JB exposed to those atrocities."

It's hard to pinpoint when we hit the low point of the tour or why we didn't leave. But it was probably near the end when we were standing in a parking lot that is believed to be paved over old graves. Everyone on the tour sensed the ground moving as the spirits wrestled right beneath our very feet. Or maybe it was the grand finale that included a photo op by a building where guests have historically seen ghosts peering from the windows after developing their film days later (talk about ghosts of the past—who even develops film anymore?).

As the tour was finishing up, my older kids ended up in the front of the group by our guide, who was busy trying to unpack their paranormal skepticism. Totally frustrated, she asked, "Why would you go on a ghost tour if you don't believe in ghosts?"

That's fair, girl. Great question.

ODD MAN OUT

It felt strange being the odd man out when it came to believing in ghosts. I realized I'm kind of used to being in the majority when it comes to my beliefs. It seems most of my time is spent around people who generally agree with my faith, who believe in my God, and who talk about supernatural acts in the heavenly realm and not so much about the chains clanging in an attic realm.

I recently ran across a Gallup poll indicating the number of people who believe in God in the United States has dipped to a new low, at 81 percent. That's still a large number of people who claim to believe in God; yet when you consider that in the 1950s and 1960s that same poll showed almost 98 percent, you can appreciate how we seem to be moving in the wrong direction.[1]

Then there's an eye-opening statistic showing, for the first time in more than eighty years, church membership has fallen below 50 percent in the United States.[2] And although church membership is not the be-all and end-all as to whether a person has faith, it's a pretty good barometer on the priority we give it.

From time to time, as I think back on that trip, I'm reminded of the tour guide asking my kids why we would go on a ghost tour if we don't believe in ghosts. She's right: Why waste your time and resources on something you don't believe in?

I think there are similar "why" faith questions we should be asking: Why are we reading the Bible if it isn't changing our lives? Why are we praying for God's plans if we're not willing to follow them? Why do we go to church if we're not going to worship? Why are we not desperately sharing Jesus if we believe He is the only way to eternal life?

WHAT'S YOUR WHY?

Sometimes otherwise ordinary moments become crossroad moments if you stop long enough to consider your why.

That happened for me a few years ago as I was driving around completely overwhelmed by all the things that "had to happen" before my kids were out for Christmas break. The holidays were about to kick off, and I had some serious work to accomplish if we were going to "pull off" Christmas.

I mean, seriously, how could we possibly celebrate the birth of our Savior without presents wrapped in coordinating paper? The perfect Christmas cards sent with the "right" holiday stamps (no thank you on the lame flag stamps at Christmastime)? A fully stocked hot chocolate bar for all the movie and puzzle nights we would be way too busy to ever enjoy? A clean house complete with perfect Christmas decor ready for a caroling party at a moment's notice?

Right there in the midst of my overwhelmedness, I sensed the Lord asking me the same question as the tour guide that day in Salem: *Why?*

Why do you prioritize your days like you do?

Why do you place such demanding expectations on yourself and your family?

Why do you feel pressured to make things look perfect and go according to plan?

Why do you live each day worried about things that won't matter eternally?

Digging deep into the why behind what you do each day is very humbling, to say the least. But it became clear that somewhere along the way I just began willy-nilly placing certain expectations on myself. Some of those expectations came from seeing everyone around me doing things a certain way, and I too wanted to look capable by having it all together. And then there were other motivations driven by the fear of missing out or just underlying discontentment that caused me to chase after things that will never bring satisfaction.

Sometimes otherwise ordinary moments become crossroad moments if you stop long enough to consider your why.

But this little exploratory exercise taught me why it's so significant to routinely ask "What's your why?"—because in a world questioning the realness of God more and more with each passing year, it's never been more critical for us to make sure our why matches up with the why of the gospel.

A little cheat sheet might look something like this:

Why do we go to church? To encourage each other to love others and do good works. Hebrews 10:24–25

Why do we seek God's plans for our lives? Only through Him do we find abundant life. John 10:10

Why do we worship? God is the creator of all things and worthy of our praise. Revelation 4:11

Why do we share our faith? We are *the* plan for spreading the gospel and telling others that Jesus alone saves. Matthew 28:18–20

Why do we read the Bible? It is God-inspired and directs us to chase after what's right and to reexamine what's wrong. 2 Timothy 3:16

Why do we live differently? We are called to be holy, or set apart, because God is holy. 1 Peter 1:15–16

I've found that once you get clarity around these foundational questions, you naturally see a shifting from the things that were once so important in everyday life to things that are important for a world that needs eternal life. You stop trying to fill the God-shaped holes in your heart with cheap substitutes that suck your time, spend your money, and leave you stressed and running.

Don't get me wrong, dishes still have to be washed, kids have to be carpooled, and Christmas trees have to look perfect (okay, maybe not). But when the mundane is allowed to trump our mission, we get into dangerous territory.

As we were leaving Salem late that night, I knew it was time to do some damage control. So I asked in my most exaggerated mom voice, "Do Yanofs believe in ghosts?" Mike knew exactly where I was headed with this and gave a decisive "Nooooooo." And then Kate dutifully jumped in with a heartfelt "No way," followed by Brett saying, "Everyone knows that ghosts are just pretend, just like on *Ghostbusters*."

But when it was JB's turn to answer the question, in his cutest little high-pitched six-year-old voice, he gave a chipper "Yep, I believe in ghosts."

As if it's not already bad enough that he thinks Jonah is the third part of the Trinity—you know, God the Father, God the Son, and Jonah. But now we've got to debunk this whole ghost situation while also explaining that the Holy "Spirit" is legit. Let's just say these ghost stories are going to haunt me for many years.

But just as confidently as we will teach JB that ghosts are not real, there is a real enemy with his sights set on doing whatever it takes to get us off mission. And his greatest success comes when we live overwhelmed lives, busy and frustrated, doing things that seem to be of greatest priority here. I've heard it said this way: "If Satan can't steal a person's salvation, he attempts to steal her effectiveness."[3]

The choice is ours: We can live each day in the grind of overflowing calendars, rushed commutes, stop-light text responses, and anxious hearts, frantically rushing around town a few weeks before Christmas (or really any time of year) heaping more on ourselves than any one person can reasonably handle. Or we can hold on to Jesus, who promises that in Him the yoke is easy and the burden is light (see Matt. 11:30). May anything short of Jesus' way be our cue to reexamine our priorities, making sure our why lines up with God's.

CHAPTER 17

When God's Quiet

MESSY TRUTH

God always shows up, but less often in the remove-the-hardship kind of way and more so in the remember-who-I-am kind of way.

*C*an we take a minute to discuss our various neighborhood websites?

At what point did the communication of relevant information within our communities become a mix between open mic night and a bad family intervention?

There's everything from bobcat sightings with detailed map coordinates to "dog on the loose" alerts, coupled with "please clean up after your pet" warnings. If you get super lucky, there's a rogue firework that gets things really hopping with the "did anyone hear gunfire" posts.

I also enjoy the "suspicious car on my street" or "your teen drives too fast" posts—because the old biddy who wrote it just stared you down coming home from Target the other day. But we just can't quit 'em, these sites, because once in a while we hit the jackpot. Like when one of my neighbors went on a rant about tweens riding battery-operated motorcycles too fast and ended her post with this little jewel: "I refuse to clean up anyone's guts on my way home from work." Alrighty then, duly noted.

My family fell prey to our own neighborhood site-mare recently. Our neighbor across the street posted a video of someone stealing their Amazon package with the title of "porch pirate." Sadly, this particular pirate was cloaked only in pajama bottoms and, even worse, was my husband. It was in fact our package that had been wrongly delivered, but even so, a doorbell video viewed by most of the neighborhood proved to be an invaluable lesson on scampering about town half-dressed.

A QUIET LITTLE CHURCH

Even with all the crazy things people tend to stir up, I love my neighborhood. There's a historic little church that sits right in the middle of our community, and it's my favorite place to go when I exercise every day (and by "every day," I mean like twice a month, and I haven't broken a sweat in years). Something about it brings me a sense of nostalgia while also reminding me of what really matters when it comes to my faith.

Picture a quaint little chapel with *Little House on the Prairie* vibes, minus that awful Nellie Oleson and the devastation of Mary's sudden-onset blindness. It sits on approximately thirteen acres of prairie land, with beautiful white shiplap that would bring tears to even Joanna Gaines's eyes. There are little steps leading up to the front porch of the church, and it's surrounded by a field of wildflowers with a windmill visible a ways off in the distance.

This little church was built in the 1890s and used as a schoolhouse and a church building by the Frankford Community. The area is surrounded by prairie land once frequented by Native Americans, and pioneers in covered wagons sought shelter and refreshment in the church. Historians say it was built by a man named Phil Hamer, who had recently lost his wife during childbirth. It stands "as a testament to the skill and artistry of a man … who in his grief created a sanctuary that continues to warm hearts and comfort souls."[1]

I think what makes this little piece of history so special, beyond the fact that it's in the middle of my bustling neighborhood, is that it's also smack-dab in the middle of the city of Dallas. It's walking distance to a country club, a quarter mile from a massive tollway, and right around the corner from retail shops and fast-food restaurants.

And with every picture I've taken of the sun setting behind this church (and there are a lot), I'm reminded of how a small church built decades ago by a man grieving the loss of his wife points me back to the Lord in the simplest but most profound of ways.

STACKING STONES

Several years ago, I was struggling through a very difficult place in life, anxiously waiting for God to work in an agonizing situation. I happened to be on one of my biannual walks by that little church when I stopped at the creek that runs behind it. For weeks I had been praying faithfully for God to resolve a struggle and to show up in big ways. But week after week He did not. I was begging others to pray diligently for God's prompt answers and direction for our family, but month after month came and went while God's voice seemed silent.

I was frustrated.

I was discouraged.

I felt alone.

And frankly, I was mad at God for promising to always walk with us but suddenly ghosting me when I needed Him the most.

So one morning I found myself on the bridge overlooking the creek behind my favorite church when the tears began to form. I hate to cry, and I surely didn't plan on doing it by myself in the middle of my neighborhood. But how can you believe your whole life that God is good, and for you, and always near when you need Him the most—yet feel completely alone in the hardest place you've ever faced?

I felt a nudge from the Lord to go down to the creek bed. I wasn't sure what was going on, but I had a sneaking suspicion that it might be about to get weird. As I was walking down by the water, my memory was flooded with all the places in Scripture where people built altars to God to memorialize the miraculous things He had done for them.

I thought about the Israelites stacking stones of remembrance by the Jordan River as a way to trigger their memories when the years passed and the memories dulled. These stones were a very tangible reminder that God is who He says and is trustworthy because He's been faithful in the past and will be again in the future.

And so in the most awkward yet purposeful way, I began picking up stones. With the first stone I was reminded of a time when my husband nearly died from meningitis and encephalitis but was healed with no residual effects. Then, as I grabbed another stone, I recalled a time when our finances were tight and the Lord gave me a job we desperately needed with flexibility to still be a mom.

I stacked two more stones for my healthy children, and another representing my marriage that is strong and true after twenty years of highs and lows. I grabbed stones for my parents, who raised me to know Jesus, and more stones for deep, godly friendships with women who make me laugh while always pointing me to the Lord. And then there were stones for the gift of writing and God's willingness to let me be a tiny part of His larger kingdom plans.

Right there next to a creek in the middle of my bustling neighborhood, I found myself building a makeshift altar with stone after stone representing the hard-fought places where God's faithfulness has marked my life. Now to be clear, the stones didn't represent times when God had shielded me from the deep struggles in this life; rather, each stone represented God's presence with me in the very midst of them.

THE POWER OF A WHISPER

Have you ever noticed that when a baby is crying loudly, lowering your voice to a whisper is far more likely to soothe her than raising your voice to drown her out? It's in the quiet where she senses our calmness and presence. That's essentially what happened with Elijah when God taught him the power of a whisper, and I've seen Him do it repeatedly in my life as well.

Stay with me here for a second. Elijah was fed up with the sacrilegious nonsense of his culture. He threw down a proverbial gauntlet to those worshipping false gods and challenged them to a fiery duel. The challenge was to take two bulls and put them on separate wood piles and then pray to see whose god would show up with fire and burn the sacrifice.

After the coin toss and the national anthem, the Baal worshippers began chanting and crying out to Baal to light a fire. Despite their most valiant efforts, nothing happened. They even cut themselves in hopes of sparking a response, but again there was nothing. Elijah, fanning the flames (or lack thereof), began taunting them by suggesting they shout a little louder because their god might be busy or deep in thought or traveling. I enjoy your moxie, Elijah.

After a commercial break and the half-time show with no fire to speak of, it was now Elijah's opportunity to prove that his God was the real deal. And so with a flair for showboating, he poured a few rounds of water on the wood stack before asking God to set it ablaze. Fire instantly came down, and the people very powerfully saw that God is who He says He is and was and always will be. The people returned to God, and the prophets of Baal were slaughtered.

As you can imagine, Elijah was on quite the high after that shakedown, and nothing could dash his spirits. Except that a few days later he got some bad news that someone wanted to kill him, and he went running as fast and far as he could from his country, his people, and his God.

The Lord very graciously pursued Elijah, feeding him and giving him some rest. But what Elijah needed more than physical and emotional provision was a spiritual reminder of his creator's presence and power—and that's exactly what he got. God told him to go stand in the mouth of a cave on a mountain so He could pass by. Elijah did as he was told. He stood there expecting God to show up in the wind, or perhaps in the earthquake, or maybe even in the fire.

But God came to Elijah in a gentle whisper.

CAVES AND CREEKS

I've always found Elijah's story a little confusing because one chapter after God uses fire to prove His deity and majesty, Elijah's running scared and questioning God's protection. He experienced no fewer than ten miracles throughout his life, yet how quickly his spirit of confidence and victory changed to one of hopelessness and defeat. It's not all that dissimilar from a girl standing by a creek questioning God's goodness after countless years of living under the umbrella of His faithfulness.

Sometimes when God gets quiet, it's our cue to follow suit. Similar to a small child crying, our Father's hushed voice causes us to lean in and listen. He's not one to compete with the noise and distraction we surround ourselves with. It's hard to hear a gentle whisper over the roar of rushed calendars, habitual scrolling, and mindless streaming.

His word to Elijah is His same word for us: *Get to a quiet place and listen for Me in the gentle whisper.*

I've found it's in those very quiet places where God shows up in the most real and tangible ways. Not typically in a remove-the-hardship kind of way but always in the remember-who-I-am kind of way. He assures us that even when a chapter of our life changes, He will not.

Very recently I went back by my favorite church and stopped on that same bridge overlooking the creek where I built the altar all those years ago. There are no longer signs of the stones I once stacked—yet the glimpses of God are still deeply etched in my story.

I was reminded that God could have fixed my situation in an instant and taken my hard place away. But I'm so glad He didn't. He taught me that He loves me enough to be less intent on relieving my pain and more interested in offering me His presence. And in a stone-by-stone stacking kind of way, I saw glimpses of how deep and wide and long and high God's love is for His people.

> *He assures us that even when a chapter of our life changes, He will not.*

Sometimes God answers our struggles with Elijah-size miracles. Maybe not the fire-dropping-from-the-heavens kind of miracles but equally powerful ones of restored health, financial provision, and adoption that are so dramatic and difficult they literally bring you to your knees.

But that's the thing about caves and creeks: sometimes our circumstances don't change but our hearts do. Which is an equally powerful response by a God who is patient enough to show us how to get quiet, wait well, and allow Him to build a long memory of His faithfulness as He passes by with the tenderness of a quiet whisper.

I'm a big believer in collecting stones of remembrance. A long memory is almost always the answer in quiet seasons. I have physical stones on my desk that remind me of answered prayers. I also have metaphorical ones like calendar reminders and Post-it notes that take me back to the places where God has been so real and present in my life.

But my very favorite stone of remembrance is a living one—our little boy who I prayed so desperately for in the middle of our foster care journey. And as I watch him learn to write his new last name or ride a bike or pray simple prayers on the way to school, I'm reminded of that time in a creek bed behind a church in the middle of my neighborhood, where I learned that the hardest moments of quiet reveal our greatest glimpses of God.

CHAPTER 18

The COVID Chronicles

MESSY TRUTH

The irony of the gospel of suffering is that
only in giving up your life can you save
it, and in the very midst of your greatest
weaknesses you find God's strength.

*T*here was a movie in the mid-'90s called *Outbreak*. The plot was about a virus originating in Africa and spreading to the United States. This virus began with flu-like symptoms but quickly progressed to become deadly. It was also highly contagious, so much so that an entire town was isolated from the rest of society because this ill-fated disease had the potential to take out an entire nation.

I never saw the movie because it was so far-fetched and unbelievable. Seriously—a deadly virus passing from a foreign country to the United States presenting with flu-like symptoms? *Typical Hollywood being out of touch with reality.*

Not to mention, the trailer for *Outbreak* showed a man coughing in a movie theater and infecting an entire roomful of people, which is just gross and freaky all at once. These are among the many reasons I don't really like science fiction. Who can even relate?

Fast-forward about twenty-five years, and my family was enjoying an early spring break at Disney World. If there's ever been a place to escape reality, it's Disney. That week we were living large on all the iconic rides and eating turkey legs. We began receiving texts from friends and family asking if we were watching the news. *Umm, no. We paid a lot of money to avoid such things, so please don't kill our Disney buzz.*

But at some point, we did hear rumblings about a pandemic potentially spreading through the US and a possibility of crowds being discouraged and international travel being suspended. I remember actually saying the words "There's just no way a pandemic could shut down our country." So we enjoyed the rest of our week and flew home only days before a pandemic did, in fact, "shut down our country."

Forever the optimist, I also assured our family at the beginning of lockdown that we were completely fine because, What could possibly happen in the safety of our own home? As fast as Lysol turned to gold, I ate those words, proving yet again that truth is stranger than fiction.

I now summarize those early pandemic days as "that time when JB broke both of his arms, I had an emergency surgery, and there was a shooting in our house right before the tree-trimming incident."

Yes, JB broke both of his arms (on two separate occasions during COVID), and I went from praying my family would rise up and call me blessed to praying nobody would call CPS. And then Brett and Mike got sick of hearing squirrels in our attic, so they put a scope on a BB gun and camped out in our attic in hopes of a squirrel showdown. Their victory against the squirrel was a loss for my bathroom ceiling (six BB holes still remain), leaving me to wonder why people get hunting leases when you can simply head to the attic.

I won't go into too much detail on my own emergency surgery, but suffice it to say that life is cruel when one day you think you're still young and hip, contemplating Coldplay tickets, and the next day you're taking advice from eighty-year-olds on recovering from gallbladder surgery.

And then there were the work disruptions. The problem with being a trial lawyer during COVID is it's tough to try cases when the courthouses are shut down. So to say Mike was getting a bit stir-crazy during lockdown would be a massive understatement. At one particularly low point in his lockdown journey, Mike declared our trees needed to be trimmed. Not those little crepe myrtle deals well within arm's reach but the big oak tree out front that normal people pay harnessed professionals with insurance to scale and trim on their behalf.

Mike dusted off his A-frame ladder and headed up the tree with neither a care in the world nor a word of warning to his family. I got wind of it about an hour later when Kate, all too casually on a stroll to the pantry, mentioned Dad was stuck in a tree. Come again?

I went outside only to find he had bitten off more than he could chew—or sawed off more than he could navigate—and the branch he had used to climb way up in our tree was now lying on the ground, leaving him no way down. To be fair, Mike insisted he was fine and there was no need to call for help. But after a lively debate over Operation Tree Trimming, we agreed to disagree. I did what any good wife does who needs her husband's brain intact for everyday living—I called 911.

I was really proud of the 911 operator, who never broke stride while having me repeat several times that my husband *was in fact stuck in a tree* (apparently that's not a call they receive often). Within minutes you could hear the siren wailing as the first responders turned into our quiet neighborhood. The same neighborhood where every single resident was home and bored and walking up and down the streets because there was nothing else to do when the world was on lockdown.

It was quite the sight when the firefighters arrived. They didn't bring just your run-of-the-mill, ordinary fire truck; nope, they were flexing with the huge one requiring a separate driver to man the back half of the engine. It took up the bigger part of a city block to park the thing, and I especially enjoyed the clown-car effect as all the firemen jumped out of the truck, ready for action. Very subtle.

They couldn't have been nicer as they pulled out their ladders and ushered my husband back down to safety. It was as if they had done it hundreds of times before (for cats), and they even repeatedly thanked us for giving the younger guys some much-needed ladder work. Kate very "graciously" videoed the whole thing, so it's forever memorialized—including my husband's post-rescue words: "I *really was* fine up there."

ISN'T THAT IRONIC?

Alanis Morissette released a song not long after that *Outbreak* movie in the '90s called "Ironic." In the song she goes through a bunch of scenarios meant to show life's ironies, but they're really not ironic—more examples of bad luck. Things like rain on your wedding day or winning the lottery and dying the next day. When asked about the irony of writing a song about irony that's not ironic at all, she jokingly said, "I'm the smartest stupid person you'll meet."[1]

I think that sums up my pandemic experience.

I found that one of the hardest parts of the pandemic was watching the world question God in the midst of such widespread suffering. At times it felt strange believing in an all-loving, all-powerful God as the world seemed to be falling apart a little more with each passing day. So many questions surfaced, asking where God was in all of this.

Honestly, there were moments I wondered too.

In the face of suffering, I'm always reminded of two of my favorite passages in all the Bible, both from the story of Job. He had just lost everything dear to him and was struggling through his hardest places of grief, and he was questioning God's justice system. God allowed Job to vent and listened in as he dialogued with his friends before beginning a beautiful response starting with three powerful words: "Where were you?"

> Where were you when I laid the earth's foundation?
>   Tell me, if you understand.
> Who marked off its dimensions? Surely you know!
>
> Who shut up the sea behind doors
>   when it burst forth from the womb,
> when I made the clouds its garment
>   and wrapped it in thick darkness,
> when I fixed limits for it
>   and set its doors and bars in place...?
>
> Have you ever given orders to the morning,
>   or shown the dawn its place,
> that it might take the earth by the edges
>   and shake the wicked out of it? (Job 38:4–5a,
>   8–10, 12–13)

These words weren't intended to be God's lesson on sarcasm but simply a word on His sovereignty. Example by example, God spoke of the complexity of our vast universe, from the galaxies and cosmos all the way down to the seasons and animals. He created all of it before even one human breath was taken, pointing out that our personal experience is small and limited. We are cautioned not to make assumptions about God's goodness based on our finite view of the world and instead reminded that glimpses of God are visible throughout creation.

Ironically, as time passed during COVID, I found it hard *not to see God* in the middle of our most difficult days. I began to sense His presence in the return of family dinners and game nights with relaxed bedtime routines. He was there in our deepest needs for community met through birthday parades and online family reunions. There were countless walks around our neighborhoods, with His presence visible in everything from nature to hopeful sidewalk-chalk messages.

We saw Him in the stories of bravery by our frontline workers, selflessly caring for the sick despite burdensome concerns for their own families. He was present in the kindness of neighbors delivering groceries to senior adults, taking care of each other in the midst of the unknown.

As time passed during COVID, I found it hard not to see God in the middle of our most difficult days.

Whether it was people connecting through the banging of pots and pans from high-rises or outdoor graduation ceremonies for graduating seniors, God's hand was all over our world in the most real and tangible ways.

As hard as those days were, I now look back a few years later and I'm reminded of Job's conversation with God during his suffering. After God gave him the "where were you" bigger perspective, Job responded with a statement of faith I've adopted after walking hard roads in my own life:

> My ears had heard of you but now my eyes have
> seen you. (Job 42:5)

What a powerful testimony that generally comes only from walking with God through hard places. It's one thing to have the head knowledge of God and hear stories of His trustworthiness no matter what we face. But it's a whole different level of faith to experience it firsthand when you're struggling through loss, hardship, and a pandemic that changed the world as we know it. Only then have you gone from *hearing* about God to very tangibly *seeing* Him for who He is.

I tease my husband for overusing a particular C. S. Lewis quote, so it pains me to now use it myself. But in *The Lion, the Witch, and the Wardrobe*, the kids ask a character who has met the lion (who represents God) whether he is "safe." The character responds:

> Who said anything about safe? 'Course he isn't
> safe. But he's good. He's the King, I tell you.[2]

Never safe but always good. It's one of the many ironies of the gospel of suffering. Other notable ironies include giving up your life so you can save it (Matt. 16:25) or finding strength when you're at your weakest (2 Cor. 12:9). The one I witnessed over and over again during COVID is the realness of joy that's found even in the face of our deepest mourning (Ps. 126:5–6).

Clearly my family struggled through the pandemic with a comedy of errors and medical messes that are hard to believe—even as one who actually lived it. I also spared you the details of the lice "situation" because there ain't nobody who wants to relive that.

But God showed up over and over again, and we experienced joy in the little things like extra family time, amazing doctors who fix broken arms and gallbladders, and even firefighters willing to assist in unlikely rescues.

My testimony is now strong: What we once knew only with our ears, we have now seen with our eyes. God's character never changes. He is good, faithful, and just as loving to us in the difficulties as in the easier times. And right there in the middle of the struggles is where we so often see how good He really is. Sustaining us. Protecting us. And delivering us.

CHAPTER 19

MESSY TRUTH

If our theology has no impact on our reality,
it's no theology at all; it's just good advice.

*I*have a sign fetish. Not *that* kind of fetish, but more of an "obsessed with" kind of fetish.

I guess if you're going to have a fetish, signs aren't a bad way to go. It beats having a foot fetish or some other weird one that at best makes you a "prayer request" in your mom's Thursday morning prayer group or at worst lands you with six weeks of community service.

There's a little Mexican restaurant in Austin that, hands down, has the best signs of all time. There's an old-timey marquee in front of their restaurant, where each week they post hilarious quips that have become local legend.

In fact, El Arroyo's signs are so epic that coffee table books, stickers, and magnets are available all over the country with their quotes. They even make snarky Christmas ornaments that I would love to give each one of you.

If you like nothing else in this book, you'll thank me for listing my top-ten favorite El Arroyo marquee quotes:

10. Unless you fell on a treadmill, nobody wants to hear about your workout.

9. Don't blame the holidays; you were fat in July.

8. If cats could text you, they wouldn't.

7. I don't always roll a joint, but when I do, it's my ankle.

6. Just told my kids I'm older than Google. They think I'm joking.

5. Website: We use cookies to improve our performance. Me: Same.

4. When this virus is over, I still want some of y'all
   to stay away from me.

3. What if soy milk is just regular milk introducing
   itself in Spanish?

2. She's a good girl, loves her llama. Loves Cheez-Its
   and asparagus too.

1. How y'all summer body lookin'? Mine's lookin'
   like I have a great personality.

I would be well served to stop here since my own words cannot possibly measure up to El Arroyo's greatness. But my publisher likely disagrees, so I'll continue.

As much as I adore El Arroyo signs, I also appreciate a good passive-aggressive sign. Some of the best ones are posted at sports complexes and go something like this:

Please remember:
   I am a kid.
   It's just a game.
   My coach is a volunteer.
   The officials are humans.
   No college scholarships will be handed out today.

I could write a whole book on crazy parents' antics at sporting events, since I've had a front row seat to watch that runaway train for years. I once asked Tony Dungy (Hall of Fame and Super Bowl–winning NFL coach, among other things) his view on youth sports, and he said, "The problem with youth sports is not the youth." Ouch!

I second that after seeing dad coaches get thrown out of little league games and seven-year-olds warned that the sport is going to pass them by if they don't work harder. And that was just my husband. My favorite was one time when I witnessed a group of softball moms line up on the third base line and dirty dance to their team's walk-up songs. Truth is stranger than fiction, people.

All that to say, I love a good sign. I especially love it when sign meets theology, or what the cool kids are now calling sign-ology. (BTW, absolutely not one single cool person has ever used the term *sign-ology*.)

I went through a serious sign-ology phase in our house. I had those little box-looking signs with meaningful sayings on all our bookshelves. One that's still hanging out in our family room says "I need Thee every hour." There's also one in our laundry room with "Pardon the mess; we're making memories here" (a nod to my first podcast).

One sign I thought was so clever said, "Be the exception." I hoped it would give my kids pause as they considered how to treat people and what they allowed to infiltrate their lives. Instead, my then middle schooler received a failing grade on a test and completely weaponized my sign with "I was just *being the exception* to good grades in this house."

That sign is now gone.

One of my favorite signs lived front and center on our coffee table and said "I remember praying for the things I have today." Oh, how quickly we take for granted today some of our biggest prayer requests from days past. But then my toddler took a Sharpie to that sign and a few of my other favorite decorative pieces, and it took every bit of my box-sign theology to keep it together.

I'm going to "pardon this mess" remembering "I once prayed for this" precious child's adoption. And I'm gonna "need Thee every hour" to help me "be the exception" to a perimenopausal crazy lady.

See how the internal dialogue works?

DOORPOST DOCTRINE

Now I know, as some of you interior designer sorts read this chapter, a little piece of you is dying because these homely little signs go against every fiber of your fabulously stylish beings. It doesn't help my case that even the Progressive insurance guy slaps a "No fussin', no cussin', no back talkin'" sign out of a girl's hand, trying to save her from becoming her parents.[1]

This idea of posting our theology for all to see isn't new, however. Take Martin Luther for example: he famously hammered his Ninety-five Theses on the doors of a church more than five hundred years ago. Our Jewish friends also have a doorpost doctrine of sorts based on a passage in Deuteronomy.

So if sign-ology is biblical and God is for me, who can stand against? (Rhetorical, thank you).

Not surprisingly, I love how the Jewish faith uses mezuzahs. I didn't know what a mezuzah was for many years, but I really enjoy saying the word. (Like that *Seinfeld* episode where Jerry talks about how fun it is to say the word *salsa*.[2] Say it with me: *salsa, saaaalsa, sa-llllll-sa*. There're so many different ways to play this thing.)

A mezuzah (the Hebrew word for "doorpost") is the small, rectangular box that many in the Jewish faith attach to the right-hand side of their front doorframe. The purpose of the mezuzah is to remind them of their covenant with God. It also signifies their Jewish beliefs to all who come into their home.

Inside the mezuzah are rolled up little scrolls with two of the most beloved Jewish prayers, both found in Deuteronomy. One is called the Shema, which is "Love the LORD your God with all your heart and with all your soul and with all your strength" (Deut. 6:5). The second prayer is a very similar passage, but it also emphasizes the importance of committing all you are to God.

Stay with me here for a second. These prayers are posted on their doorposts for a couple of reasons. First, God very practically instructs the Israelites to obey His commandments by ingraining them in their hearts and teaching them to their children when they wake up, when they are at home, and when they are out and about. That's pretty much the best parenting advice you'll ever get—teach your kids the God-stuff at every feasible point in your day, no matter the time and no matter the place.

Second, God—knowing how quickly our thoughts are prone to wander and our allegiances to waver—literally instructs the Israelites to put reminders of Him on their doorposts so they might follow His Word and keep His commandments.

Some devout Jews even have a mezuzah over each door inside their house, touching it every time they enter or leave a room. I envision it being the spiritual equivalent to the locker room sign "Clear eyes, full hearts, can't lose" (but nobody would liken it to *Friday Night Lights* because that would be weird).[3]

I especially love how the Hebrew word *shin*, representing *Shaddai* or *God,* is visible on the front of the mezuzah—a reminder of who is most important in our lives while also causing me to hum an Amy Grant song from my youth. IYKYK.

So if you see a mezuzah over a family's doorpost, let it remind you of their commitment to keeping God visible in their home and His Word unmistakably central to their lives.

Similarly, if you see an ugly box sign in my house, be reminded that sometimes ugly is biblical, so let's just keep our preciousness to ourselves.

PREACHING TO OURSELVES

I like to think of the mezuzah as God's reminder to preach little sermons to ourselves throughout the day. There isn't a day that passes when I don't need a mezuzah sermon over my own door, reminding me that, at my very core, I'm called to love God and love others freely and unconditionally.

That sermon alone should be enough to keep me on track. But I've found that even as I begin most days grounded in God's Word, by lunchtime I'm grounded in everything from workplace gossip to baseball-field injustices to financial discontentment. So often my theology doesn't line up with my reality, making little signs or sticky notes or mezuzahs much-needed reminders as I go throughout my day.

After all, if our Father in heaven alone knows what our future holds, we would be well served to remember His marching orders as we head out into an unknown world.

I have a friend who tells the story of waking up one morning with the gut sense that she needed to teach her small children how to dial 911. Anyone who has raised preschoolers understands there's a slippery slope between teaching them safety protocols and the possibility that you'll step out of the shower in a towel wrap with two firefighters and a paramedic standing in your bedroom. It could go either way.

But my friend sensed an urgency (let's call that the Holy Spirit) to teach her kids about 911 that very day. So she dropped what she was doing and got a little dry-erase board and wrote the numbers 9-1-1 on her sign. She then sat her little girls down and began explaining how it works, practicing with her cell phone and even rehearsing the specific information to relay depending on the scenario. Clearly, she raises more attentive and responsible preschoolers than I do.

Later that same day, while my friend was still home alone with her two little girls, she had a massive seizure. This was her first seizure ever, so it was unexpected to say the least. The oldest of her two young daughters immediately ran back to their playroom to grab the dry-erase board, looking for the instructions her mom had taught them earlier that morning. With her sign in hand, she grabbed her mom's phone and successfully called 911 with the lifesaving instructions she had recently learned.

That's what spending time with God looks like. It's giving Him a few minutes to write His most critical information on our metaphorical dry-erase boards each day. It's His loving way of preparing us for when the school calls or the pink slip drops or the diagnosis is confirmed.

But here's the rub: So often the instructions don't make sense in the moment God gives them. The information feels irrelevant or even outdated in our high-tech, agenda-oriented, overscheduled

If our Father in heaven alone

knows what our future holds,

we would be well served

to remember His marching

orders as we head out into

an unknown world.

lives. We don't have the context to appreciate its value, and we slip into the trap of thinking our time is better spent focusing on the everyday practical rather than the desperately needed spiritual.

Yet our naivety doesn't change God's urgency. Just as my friend knew the value of teaching her daughters a lesson they couldn't fully understand in the moment, God is intent on doing the same for us.

WHAT'S ON YOUR SIGN?

Yes, I've had a sign fetish for years. Between you and me, perhaps it's been borderline unhealthy and largely unsightly at times. But I understand the value in having God's reminders on our doorposts or in the laundry room or even on the living room shelves (yep, I said it). Because sometimes the message is universal—like calling 911 in an emergency—but other times it's very personal.

I like to picture God sitting down with me, holding a dry-erase board and a marker, listing out His most lifesaving and life-giving instructions for my life. Many of the lessons probably won't make complete sense to me today, but I know one day they will because I sense the urgency with which He's teaching these lessons over and over again.

I think God's white board sign-ology to me would read something like this:

- God above all else, no matter what.
- Your story isn't finished.
- Do the hard things.

- If I am for you, stop focusing on who is not.
- People are the priority (even those you find mean or annoying).
- Your actions always speak louder than your words.
- Be a yes when everyone else around you says no.
- Build a life that's interruptible.

(Can someone please ask Hobby Lobby to make this sign for me—and also maybe put this book on their darling front shelves if it's not too much trouble?)

Netting it out: If our theology has no impact on our reality, it's no theology at all; it's just good advice. God's not in the business of good advice; He's in the business of changing lives. So the question becomes: What's your sign-ology?

CHAPTER 20

Life in a Dirty Suit

MESSY TRUTH

Each day we have an invitation to get dirty in
this life by doing the hard and messy things—not
for earthly recognition, but for heavenly.

Recently I was having lunch with a group of friends I had just met during a weekend writers' retreat. We were making small talk about various things when someone suggested we go around the table and name the person who has had the most impact on our lives. This conversation went deep fast, considering I had just been zoned out thinking about the awesome mah-jong scene in *Crazy Rich Asians*.

The only parameter given was that it couldn't be Jesus, because this group of amazing godly women (and me) would have immediately gone there, and it would have been a short conversation. Not that Jesus lends Himself to short conversations, but if you've made it this far in this book, you know what I mean.

Thankfully, it was a large group of women at lunch that day, and they started at the opposite end from where I was seated, so I was last in line to share. I was grateful to have plenty of time to think about my answer while also listening to beautiful stories of people who had profoundly impacted each of these women.

As I was considering who I was going to talk about, I immediately thought of my mom and dad. I've talked over and over about how unconditionally they have loved me every single day of my life. They've faithfully pointed me to Jesus while also pointing me away from things that would harm me. There's really nobody like my amazing parents.

And then there's Mike and my kids, who have made my life the sweetest, most incredible adventure one could ever ask for this side of heaven. (They've also almost driven me to my grave at times, but I guess that's the price of having a precious family.)

I thought about my friend Brandie, who time and time again has believed in me when I haven't believed in myself. She has prayed for me (I mean *really, really* prayed for me) when I didn't know how to pray for myself and has wholeheartedly declared in faith that God will use this book in mighty ways.

Then there's Stephanie, who loves me enough to say what I don't want to hear. She has the most amazing gift of discernment and teaches me daily how to live authentically for Jesus. She calls it what it is (and sometimes what it is kills me), but there's nobody else I would rather walk through life with.

And then I thought of my sweet Marianne, who's the sister God never gave me. I may not even know you, but I can say with 100 percent certainty you would love her. She's funny, godly, irreverent, fashionable, and everything I stand for when it comes to friendship. And her husband works for an airline, so fun trips and fabulousness come with the territory of this soul sister.

As I sat there thinking of who had most impacted my life, I quickly realized I couldn't narrow it down to one single person. It's this beautiful, cumulative effect of so many people whom the Lord has placed around me the last fifty years who have individually and uniquely shaped every itsy-bitsy tiny little speck of who I am today. I'm just so grateful.

So when it came to my turn, instead of sharing the one *person* who has most impacted my life, I decided I would share the one *story* that has most marked my life. And it's this same story I want to share with you as I wrap up a book filled with chapters about my life, my faith, and all the messy parts we walk together on the road toward Jesus.

WHERE HAVE YOU BEEN?

Mike and I have a friend who works as a Secret Service agent. I know, right?

Try comparing war stories about carpool lines or mah-jong with a guy who's literally protected many of the leaders of the free world. He's never given us details on his assignments—I'm assuming it's the whole "I could tell you but then I'd have to kill you" thing—but suffice it to say he's been assigned to countless dignitaries, ambassadors, and presidents over the years.

This friend also happened to be in New York City the morning of September 11, 2001. He was there on assignment with the Secret Service, meeting in their offices at 7 World Trade Center. Just as each of us remembers some of the finer details from that morning as we heard the shocking news of 9/11, Darin remembers being dressed in a business suit, meeting with members of the agency, preparing for a busy week of assignments.

Then the first plane hit the North Tower.

Darin said they knew instantly it was a terrorist attack, and he and a few colleagues ran out of the building toward the North Tower to see how they might possibly help.

I must pause here to tell you that Darin is *incredibly* humble, and it's basically pulling teeth to get him to share details from this part of the story. I also have to tell you that he received a Secret Service Medal of Valor for his response to the 9/11 tragedies, so every bit of the acknowledgment he receives is unquestionably well deserved.

Darin and a friend arrived at the North Tower and began helping injured people on the streets the best they knew how. Soon thereafter, a second plane hit the South Tower, further confirming what they already understood to be a terrorist attack and giving them increased urgency in their evacuation efforts. Darin and two other agents entered the North Tower and climbed the stairwells, helping as many people to safety as they could.

Thankfully, they escaped before the North Tower crumbled to the ground, but Darin recalls running as fast as he possibly could while debris and smoke chased them and countless others block after block. He also talks about seeing the faintest bit of light on the horizon of Manhattan that day and yelling to those around him to run to the light to save their lives.

Don't gloss over this. When everything looked chaotic, dark, and perilous, Darin knew their only hope was to run to the light. That preaches a sermon right there in and of itself.

After they reached safety and the dust began to settle, Darin headed back to the South Tower to once again help with evacuations and anything else he might be able to assist with. He did makeshift paramedic work helping some of the injured individuals he saw on each block. It was only a matter of time before the South Tower collapsed too, leaving thousands of people once again running from the cloud of debris that made it near impossible to breathe, let alone see far enough to find safety.

The remainder of their day was spent putting out small ancillary fires, using fire trucks and other equipment left abandoned in the streets. He remembers at one point questioning where all the firefighters were before realizing they were likely heroically rescuing people at the time the buildings collapsed.

But here's the part of the story that has marked me from the first time I heard it: At the end of a horrific day of terrorist acts taking so many innocent lives, Darin made his way to an emergency relocation point where the Secret Service was reconvening (because their offices at 7 World Trade Center had been destroyed). After a day of aiding in evacuations, assisting in basic medical care, and putting out small fires around the sacred area we now call ground zero, you can imagine how Darin looked walking into the room.

He was bloody from all the flying debris, and his face was black from the soot in the air. His clothes were ripped. And his shoes were literally melted on his feet from the heat he experienced that day.

As he walked into a roomful of Secret Service agents at the end of an unspeakable day, he faced many of the same men from earlier that morning. Taken aback by his appearance, several asked, "Where have you been?"

Looking at the room of agents—over half still in their same clean suits from earlier that morning—Darin thought, *No, where have you been?*

You see, Darin chooses to live a life that does not end with a clean suit. He's made the decision to live fully and freely for Jesus, pursuing what the Lord puts in his path no matter the cost. He goes full speed toward the hard, overlooked, and dangerous things that just may leave him beaten up and bruised. But he does so knowing God is with him and that a safe and sterile life could never be enough.

Obviously, Darin didn't know his actions on 9/11 would earn him a Medal of Valor; that never would have entered his mind. It's not the earthly recognition he's after, it's the heavenly. And if living a life that's dangerous and dirty—loving people and risking his life for those who may never have the opportunity to thank him in return—earns him a heavenly "well done" from his Savior, that's exactly what he's set out to do.

THE BIG AND SMALL OF IT ALL

I think this story has marked me because it sums up my hope for my own life. It's my prayer for your life as well: That we would be uncompromising in our commitment to get dirty in this life, doing the hard, messy, and oftentimes unappreciated things. We do it not for earthly recognition, but heavenly.

And just as you've read my personal stories of foster care, living anointed, losing a dear friend, and even loving church people when it hurts … my deepest desire is for you to see how these stories are not just my stories but *ours*. Each and every story we write in our lives—the big, small, funny, ridiculous, mundane, and gut-wrenching—is a part of God's bigger story. Because God is right there with us.

He's there when our finances get tight and our marriages are hard. He's there when our friends disappoint and our kids struggle with addiction.

And it's in every one of these dirty-suit moments when we have the opportunity to live boldly and with confidence. These are our

Each and every story we write

in our lives—the big, small,

funny, ridiculous, mundane,

and gut-wrenching—is a part

of God's bigger story. Because

God is right there with us.

moments to see that God is on every road with us, directing us as we walk this impossibly messy journey.

I think my greatest joy would be if one day, when we pass each other at a baseball game or at a take-out restaurant after the longest day ever, we could share a simple-but-knowing smile saying *Yes, life is messy and hard and devastating, and some days feel like more than we can possibly handle. But God is good, and He's right here with us. He is today, He was yesterday, and He always will be.*

Turns out life really *is* messy, but God *is* good.

Acknowledgments

I'll never forget the first day of law school, when my naive little twenty-something-year-old self sat in my first orientation meeting and heard a professor use an age-old scare tactic. He told us to look to our left and our right and notice the people on either side of us. He went on to say that in three years, when law school was over, only one of us would still be sitting there. The idea was to generate a competitive spirit by pointing out that the journey would be hard and most would not complete it. I'm happy to report that I was still sitting there three years later, barely.

I think about my life today, and I can't help but once again stop and consider the people to my left and my right. Being a lot further down the road than my twenty-year-old self was all those years ago in law school, I've learned that those closest to us are not the competition but part of a bigger collaboration. And to say this book has been my life's biggest collaboration … well, that's a massive understatement.

So thank you to all who have supported me, laughed with (and at) me, pointed me to Jesus, and lived stories worthy of retelling. Bear with me as I acknowledge just a few of those who are consistently in my corner:

Before there were editors assigned to this book, there was **my husband, Mike**. Over the last year he has read, reread, edited, suggested, and reworked this book tirelessly. Is he a little too loose with a red pen and ridiculously committed to proper grammar? Sure. But his attention to detail and heart for helping me fulfill this book dream is a very tangible act of his selfless love. Thank you.

If it's true that "what doesn't kill you makes you stronger," then **Kate, Brett, and JB** have given me Herculean strength. Their irreverent humor and over-the-top antics are the greatest gift a mom could ever ask for. Don't settle for the easy path guys; keep chasing after the God-sized dreams (and I'll keep writing embarrassing stories about you).

When you're a super regular person, it's borderline ridiculous to mention you have an agent. So let's just say I'm very fortunate to have **Eric Wolgemuth** in my court as a friend, ally, advocate and, yes, agent. Eric gave me the shot that most probably would not have, especially when I showed up with one single chapter about a French fry and a scarf. Thanks for believing before seeing. Here's to praying it pays off.

To **Sharon, April, my heavenly Elaine, Sherry, Mom, Dad, Curtis, Cory, Mike, Kate, Brett, JB, Pastor Pierre, David Green, "Besties," and the "Wednesday Lunchers"**: Thank you for allowing me to include your stories. But even more than that, thank you for living boldly enough to create stories worth sharing.

And to **Darin Kinder**, who graciously allowed me to end this book with a portion of his sacred 9/11 story: The call to live with a "dirty suit" has changed me, and I can't wait for your upcoming book and TheValiantMinistries.com to change many, many more lives.

To **Susan McPherson and the Esther Press folks:** Wow, what a fun and crazy journey this has been. Let's be clear, I don't want to know if you're questioning the two-book deal now that we're dragging ourselves over the book-one finish line. But I promise to act more like a real author for book two and be lower maintenance with all my questions. And to Susan McPherson specifically, you are my people. Book or no book, I'm better now because of your friendship.

Notes

INTRODUCTION

1. *Talladega Nights: The Ballad of Ricky Bobby*, directed by Adam McKay (Culver City, CA: Sony Pictures Entertainment, 2006).

CHAPTER 1

1. Rick Warren, "Learn How to Live the Anointed Life" (sermon, Saddleback Church, Lake Forest, CA, May 23, 2017), www.youtube.com/watch?v =GOvTfCATkBE.

2. Anne Graham Lotz, Denison Forum conference (speaker, The Cove, Asheville, NC, October 27–29, 2017).

CHAPTER 2

1. The B-52s, "Love Shack," by Kate Pierson, Fred Schneider, Keith Strickland, and Cindy Wilson, released June 1989 on *Cosmic Thing*, Dreamland Recording.

2. *The Wiersbe Bible Commentary: New Testament*, 2nd ed. (Colorado Springs, CO: David C Cook, 2007), 1043.

CHAPTER 6

1. Horatio Spafford, hymnist, and Philip Bliss, composer, "It Is Well with My Soul," *Gospel Hymns, No. 2*, 1876, public domain.

CHAPTER 7

1. Marvin Gaye, vocalist, "Sexual Healing," by Marvin Gaye, Odell Brown, David Ritz, released October 1982 on *Midnight Love*, Columbia/CBS Records.

CHAPTER 8

1. Mark Batterson, *In a Pit with a Lion on a Snowy Day: How to Survive and Thrive When Opportunity Roars* (Colorado Springs, CO: Multnomah, 2016), 16.

2. Phil Wickham, vocalist, "Battle Belongs," by Phil Wickham and Brian Johnson, released September 2020 on *Hymn of Heaven*, Fair Trade Music.

3. Mark Batterson, *Wild Goose Chase: Reclaim the Adventure of Pursuing God* (Colorado Springs, CO: Multnomah, 2008), 122.

CHAPTER 9

1. Francis Chan, *Crazy Love: Overwhelmed by a Relentless God* (Colorado Springs, CO: David C Cook, 2013), 131.

2. Laura Carrione, "Hobby Lobby Founder Explains Decision to 'Give Away Ownership' of Company: 'Joy in Giving What We Have,'" Fox Business, November 14, 2022, www.foxbusiness.com/retail/hobby-lobby-founder-explains-decision-give-away-ownership-company-joy-giving.

3. Brian Solomon, "Meet David Green: Hobby Lobby's Biblical Billionaire," *Forbes*, October 7, 2012, www.forbes.com/sites/briansolomon/2012/09/18/david-green-the-biblical-billionaire-backing-the-evangelical-movement.

CHAPTER 12

1. Anthony O'Reilly, "Muscle Memory: What It Is and How to Use It," Trifecta Nutrition, June 27, 2020, www.trifectanutrition.com/blog/muscle-memory -what-is-it-how-to-use-it.

2. A. W. Tozer, *The Pursuit of God*, in *The Essential Tozer Collection*, James L. Snyder, ed. (Bloomington, MN: Bethany House, 2017), 77.

CHAPTER 13

1. David Brooks, "Five Lies Our Culture Tells," *New York Times*, April 15, 2019, www.nytimes.com/2019/04/15/opinion/cultural-revolution-meritocracy.html.

2. Mike Yanof, "Ordinary Events Made Extraordinary" (unpublished manuscript, May 20, 2019).

CHAPTER 14

1. *Merriam-Webster*, s.v. "salvation", accessed May 4, 2023, www.merriam -webster.com/dictionary/salvation.

2. Lysa TerKeurst, *Forgiving What You Can't Forget: Discover How to Move On, Make Peace with Painful Memories, and Create a Life That's Beautiful Again* (Nashville, TN: Thomas Nelson, 2020), xvi.

CHAPTER 15

1. S. J. Scott, "55 Famous Failures Who Became Successful People," Develop Good Habits, July 12, 2020, www.developgoodhabits.com/successful-people-failed.

2. Scott, "55 Famous Failures," www.developgoodhabits.com/successful -people-failed.

CHAPTER 16

1. Lydia Saad and Zach Hrynowski, "How Many Americans Believe in God?," Gallup, June 24, 2022, https://news.gallup.com/poll/268205/americans-believe -god.aspx.

2. Jeffrey M. Jones, "U.S. Church Membership Falls Below Majority for First Time," Gallup, March 29, 2021, https://news.gallup.com/poll/341963/church -membership-falls-below-majority-first-time.aspx.

3. Joe Beam, *Seeing the Unseen: Preparing Yourself for Spiritual Warfare* (New York: Howard, 2000), 184.

CHAPTER 17

1. Kathy Power, "The Frankford Church," Frankford Preservation Foundation website, accessed May 4, 2020, https://frankfordpreservationfoundation.org /the-frankford-church.

CHAPTER 18

1. Sophie Heawood, "Alanis Morissette: I'm the smartest stupid person you'll meet," *London Times*, June 14, 2008, www.thetimes.co.uk/article/alanis -morissette-im-the-smartest-stupid-person-youll-meet-qmscxbqjhrf.

2. C. S. Lewis, *The Lion, the Witch, and the Wardrobe* (Springfield, OH: Collier Books, 1970), 75–76.

CHAPTER 19

1. "Dr. Rick Methods Progressive Insurance," September 2, 2021, BOBAC, YouTube video, 0:27, www.youtube.com/watch?v=Kc-CN53147Q.

2. *Seinfeld*, season 4, episode 3, "The Pitch," directed by Tom Cherone, written by Larry David, Jerry Seinfeld, and Peter Mehlman, featuring Jerry Seinfeld, Julia Louis-Dreyfus, and Michael Richards, aired September 16, 1992, on NBC.

2. *Friday Night Lights*, season 1, episode 1, "Pilot," directed by Peter Berg, written by Peter Berg and Buzz Bissinger, featuring Kyle Chandler, Connie Britton, and Gaius Charles, aired October 3, 2006, on NBC.

Cynthia Yanof

If you enjoyed *Life is Messy, God is Good*, keep the momentum going!

Life's too short to take yourself seriously.
Cynthia is all too aware of this, and would love to meet
you, laugh with you, and hear your funniest stories over a bowl of queso.

How can we make this happen? Thanks for asking!

Invite her to speak at your event.

She loves to bring humor and authenticity to all subjects, but
especially parenting, prayer, foster care, doing the hard things, and
navigating the bumps and bruises of everyday life.

Listen to the *MESSmerized* podcast.

Whatever mess you're walking through,
odds are Cynthia is right there with you.
Tune in to *MESSmerized* each week for
funny, real, and vulnerable conversations
with a variety of guests. Available
wherever you listen to podcasts.

Connect with her at cynthiayanof.com or on social media @cynthiayanof.

Email her directly at cynthia@cynthiayanof.com. She would love
to know how *Life is Messy, God is Good* spoke to you.